PRICE GUIDE TO

Coca-Cola

TRADE MARK ®

COLLECTIBLES

PRICE GUIDE TO

Coca-Cola

TRADE MARK ®

COLLECTIBLES

Deborah Goldstein Hill

Contents

To my father, Sheldon Goldstein, for his dedicated commitment to gathering the finest collection of Coca-Cola memorabilia in the world. For over a decade, he spent the better part of every day corresponding with collectors. It was his devotion and excitement that stimulated the widespread interest in the field of Coke collectibles.

Acknowledgments

First, I would like to thank my husband, Arthur. It was his confidence in me that encouraged the undertaking of this project. He was forever supportive, guiding me through every step in preparing this book, including taking the photograph for the cover. To Arthur, all my love.

A special thanks to the rest of my family, too, including my mother, Helen, and my sisters, Jenifer, Lisa, and Ele Ann.

Thanks also to Peter Holden, who helped prepare the history section. His ability to condense large volumes of material accurately in a short time enabled me to meet my deadline. I would also like to thank Alan Baer and the staff at Calamity Jane's and Sam's Town for their hospitality, to all of the people from the Cola Clan who have made writing this book so pleasurable, to Steven Howard for his special care in reading and editing the manuscript, to Bob Anderson and Alison Frankley, my two best friends, who showed continuing support, to Gail Fakes, mostly for her love and interest, but also for her suggestion that I get a computer before I start this book, and to my neighbors, Scott, Jim, and Michelle, for their constant interruptions.

Finally, thanks also to the Coca-Cola Company, for over one hundred years of great advertising. I would also like to recognize Phil Mooney, Archives, Coca-Cola Company, Atlanta, Georgia, the many Coca-Cola bottlers across the country who have sent me information, Bob Buffaloe, the founder of the Cola Clan, and Sally Lorey and Alice Fisher for their contributions.

To the contributors of the Cola Clan's publication, *The Cola Call,* and to Cecil Munsey, for his work in the field of Coke memorabilia, a special thank-you. And, finally, special thanks to Candy Skinner.

Introduction

Certainly Coca-Cola advertising memorabilia is the most widely collected of all advertising collectibles. And it's little wonder when you consider the monumental quantity of items produced. Only Coca-Cola advertising memorabilia provides such an entertaining and idealistic panorama of American history.

I've often wondered how it would be to live in a time when a Coca-Cola cost only a nickel, when gas cost less than twenty-five cents a gallon, and a trip to the soda fountain was the main event of the day. It is a different world now. Ice-cold Coke now pops out of a talking vending machine that requires two quarters, and real soda fountains have become a rarity.

People will collect almost anything full of memories—baseball cards, bottle caps, or old dolls. My husband collects old cameras. Others may prefer political buttons, bottles, stamps, or coins.

This book has been prepared especially for those wonderful collectors who have been bitten by the "bug" for Coca-Cola collecting, or would like to be. It represents a century's worth of memories from the world's largest soft drink company.

Enjoy!

The creation of the most famous soft drink

In the spring of 1886, John Styth Pemberton was cooking up the first batch of what was to become Coca-Cola. Mixing the syrup in a three-legged iron kettle in the back yard of his Atlanta, Georgia, home, Pemberton experimented with what he foresaw as a headache remedy and "tonic stimulant." Clearly, John Pemberton could have had no idea that his formula would become the base of the most popular soft drink in the world.

Born in 1833, John Pemberton grew up and was educated in Columbus, Ohio. Part of his education consisted of an apprenticeship in pharmaceuticals. After the Civil War, Pemberton moved to Atlanta where he established himself as a druggist and pharmaceutical chemist. He became known for his original compounds advertised as health supplements and cures for various common ailments. Indeed, the precursor to Coca-Cola was a mixture designed to cure headaches. Pemberton patented this mixture in 1885 and called it French Wine Coca. By taking out the wine and adding a pinch of caffeine, extract of cola, and other ingredients, Pemberton formulated an as yet unnamed syrup, eventually the base of the now-famous Coke.

Shortly after its creation in May of 1886, Pemberton took a jug of his new syrup to Willis Venable, the manager of the largest soda fountain in Atlanta. Venable liked the taste when he mixed the syrup with water and agreed to sell the drink at his soda fountain.

A few months later, the story has it, a new soda clerk accidentally mixed the syrup with soda water. Thus, Coca-Cola as we know it was born. The name Coca-Cola was given to the drink after its popularity had grown and was chosen because it was an appealing alliterative combination of two of the drink's ingredients. Although ill health soon forced Pemberton to sell the rights to his new product, the special blend of ingredients basically has remained unchanged. Pemberton died in August of 1888 without seeing the complete success of his creation, but it is certain that he knew something of the value of the drink he had first made in a three-legged iron kettle two years earlier.

Turning great taste into an empire

On August 30, 1888, two weeks after the death of John S. Pemberton, Asa Griggs Candler acquired the remaining one-third of Coca-Cola stock for a mere one thousand dollars. Candler had become the controlling owner in the months prior to Pemberton's death and these final shares made him Coca-Cola's sole proprietor. Candler had spent a total of $2,300 on the rights to the soft drink that he would soon lead from obscurity to national prominence.

Asa Candler was born on December 30, 1851, near Villa Rica, Georgia. Although the Civil War had disrupted his education and had left him with only seven years of formal schooling, Candler became an apprentice to two doctors when he was nineteen years old. While he was unable to achieve his dream of becoming a doctor, Candler was able to amass a working knowledge of pharmaceuticals. In 1873, he moved to Atlanta where he was able to put this knowledge to work at the Pemberton-Pulliam Drug Store.

After building up a reputation and some capital, Candler and a partner started their own retail and wholesale drug business. The business suffered when their building was destroyed by fire. They purchased Pemberton, Iverson, and Denison, a drug company with which they could service their accounts.

Soon Candler became the sole owner of the company, and in August of 1888, he acquired the exclusive rights to Coca-Cola. Realizing its potential, Candler dropped all of his other products in order to concentrate on the soft drink. The decision proved to be a profitable one, as the company showed a $100,000 gross profit each of its first two years.

In 1892, Candler incorporated. He sold an initial 500 shares for $100 apiece. If you had been lucky enough to have acquired one of Candler's original shares of stock for $100, that same share would have been worth $17,000 in 1914.

In succeeding years, the Coca-Cola Company expanded enormously. Branch offices were opened in Dallas, Chicago, and Los Angeles. In 1909, the Atlanta operation moved into a huge, new building at the corner of Marietta and Magnolia Streets.

Candler stepped down as president of the company in 1916. It is obvious that his strength and dedication started Coca-Cola on its path toward success. During his reign, the Coca-Cola Company became one of the most successful businesses in the country.

Let's bottle it!

In the first years of Coca-Cola's existence, the popular beverage could be found only at the local soda fountain. It was not until the summer of 1894 that Joseph Biedenharn began to bottle Coke, the soft drink that was selling so well in his Vicksburg, Mississippi, store.

Biedenharn, a native of Vicksburg, was born December 13, 1866. As a teenager, Biedenharn joined his father's firm, which sold fruits, nuts, and candies. Eventually, he took over the company and moved it into a large building in Vicksburg. The success of his business allowed him to run both a retail candy shop-soda fountain as well as a wholesale candy and nut warehouse. In 1890, a Coca-Cola salesman persuaded Biedenharn to offer Coke at his soda fountain.

The Biedenharn Candy Company began bottling soda water in 1891, and three years later, introduced Coke by the bottle. The idea behind this innovation was to make Coke available to people who did not live near soda fountains.

The original Coke bottle had a six-ounce capacity and cost seventy cents for a case wholesale (compared to sixty cents for a case of regular soda water). Soon Biedenharn was delivering bottled Coca-Cola throughout the Vicksburg area and by boat up and down the Mississippi River. When he died in 1952, Joseph Biedenharn had been a Coca-Cola bottler for fifty-eight years.

Coca-Cola bottles

Since Coca-Cola was not originally created to be sold as a bottled soft drink, the founders could not have perceived the enormous potential in bottling their beverage.

Biedenharn was already bottling other drinks when he began bottling Coke. Bottles were used interchangeably, so the first Coke bottles did not bear the drink's distinctive logo. The short, six-ounce bottles used the popular Hutchinson stopper. This type of bottle top was rather bulky and consisted of a rubber gasket held between two metal plates attached to a spring wire stem. The bottles were identified only by the embossments "Registered" and "Bidenharn Candy Co., Vicksburg, Miss."

One of the central problems in the bottling industry before the turn of the century was finding a suitable bottle closure. There were hundreds invented during this period, including the Hutchinson stopper, but none was completely without problems. The main objection to the Hutchinson top was the fact that its rubber gasket became odorous and unsanitary if the bottle were not opened in about two weeks.

In 1891, William Painter of Baltimore, Maryland, invented what was to become the most practical and popular bottle top of the first half of the twentieth century—the crown cork. Although Coca-Cola did not make the crown cork mandatory with its bottlers until the emergence of its standardized bottle in 1916, this bottle closure marked an era of new sophistication in the bottling industry.

From "Deliciously Refreshing" to "Coke Is It" in seventy-five years

"The Pause That Refreshes." "It's the Real Thing!" "Things Go Better with Coke!" By the immediate familiarity of these phrases, it is clear that the promotion and advertising of Coca-Cola has been enormously successful. And, although John Styth Pemberton's syrup makes an undeniably great beverage, quality advertising has been a major force in turning Coca-Cola into the world's most popular soft drink. This success can be attributed in part to the continuity of the advertising principles initiated over seventy-five years ago by Asa Candler and W. C. D'Arcy.

Since the first Coca-Cola advertisements of the 1880s and 1890s, beautiful and elegant men and women have been shown in settings that the public admires and aspires toward. In its advertising, the Coca-Cola Company has presented itself as standing for quality, decency, wholesomeness, and, most important, the American way of life. Coca-Cola has always strived to align itself with the goodness of America and its people.

These principles are clearly seen even in the first lithographs of pretty, wholesome girls drinking Coke from Asa Candler's era. By the turn of the century, however, that medium was becoming obsolete and four-color advertisements were present in magazines. At that point, Candler decided to hand the growing task of representation over to the Massengale Advertising firm.

Massengale took over in the early 1900s, but their tenure was short-lived and their advertising pieces are now considered rare. In general, their advertisements showed beautiful people drinking Coke and playing what were then the sports of the rich—tennis, golf, and swimming.

In 1906, W. C. D'Arcy became Coca-Cola's advertising agency. Idea man Archie Lee and Coca-Cola President Robert Woodruff developed and produced ideas and copy that conveyed the image of clean Americana in the tradition that Asa Candler had begun. The look was generally the same, with wholesome and active men and women. The focus of the D'Arcy advertisements began to shift subtly towards the growing middle class. Their ideas were simple, always associating Coca-Cola with pleasant surroundings.

After both Woodruff and Lee retired, the Coca Cola Company changed advertising agencies after having been with D'Arcy for over 50 years. McKann-Ericson took over in 1956, and though not immediately successful, they have persisted against new competition from other soft drinks up to the present, and Coke is still the best selling soft drink. Though the emergence of Pepsi and others have brought the comparative element into advertising ("There's Nothing Like Coke") McKann-Ericson's biggest success was their campaign emphasizing peace, brotherhood, and Coke, which started in the early 1970s.

The song "I'd Like To Buy The World A Coke" was written by McKann-Ericson's Bill Backer. In the annual report of 1982, Coca-Cola states, "The company's most successful advertising campaign ever developed for Coca-Cola— Coke is it!—achieved record consumer awareness.

In 1983, with over two million dollars in gross profits, the company introduced the most significant product addition in ninety six years, Diet Coke—a collaboration of the world renown trademark with a great tasting, low calorie soda. The Diet Coke formula was formulated while trying to improve the once popular Tab. Ira C. Herbert, Coca-Cola USA president, said in an interview, "There's no question that the strength of the trademark is a key factor to its success." Diet Coke has become the biggest soft drink introduction of the past decade.

The tremendous appeal of Coke, caffeine free Coke, Coca-Cola Classic and Cherry Coke has allowed Coca-Cola to branch into other business markets, such as Coca-Cola Foods, which includes Minute Maid and Hi-C. Coca-Cola derives over 75% of its soft drink operating income from international operations in over 160 countries. In January 1990 the Coca-Cola trademark lighted Pushkin Square, becoming the first neon advertisement in Moscow. Two months later the most recognizable name in the world was on demand in East Berlin. As the wall came down, Coca-Cola found itself with the most exciting opportunity for the 1990s as it enters a new world behind the wall. With the political unrest in South Africa, the company divested its remaining interest in bottling and canning assets. The company will focus its energy toward increasing soft drink availability, affordability and acceptability to consumers worldwide. Catch the wave!

Starting a collection

Collecting Coca-Cola memorabilia allows a collector a great freedom for expansion and a wide variety of categories from which to choose. A collector may already have Coca-Cola items within his specialized collection. For example, there are many people who collect toys and trucks. Finding that they have several Coca-Cola items within their collections, they expand from there.

Other people like variety and collect every type of Coke memorabilia. We have everything from change trays and a pewter glass holder to a six-foot-long sign that hangs in my husband's studio.

There are also people who specialize in a particular category within Coca-Cola memorabilia. There is a man in Kentucky who has acquired over 100 different blotters during the last decade.

In the early 1960s, my parents began collecting Vienna art plates. My father was attracted by the beautiful women who adorned the plates. Western Coca-Cola Bottling Company was one of the many companies that used these art plates to promote their product. While vacationing in Solvang, Cali-

fornia, my parents ran across an ice cream parlor similar to Calamity Jane's in Las Vegas. My parents reminisced as they viewed the many serving trays displayed. It was then that they decided to build a collection of Coca-Cola serving trays.

They started searching antiques stores, particularly those specializing in advertising antiques. They attended antiques shows, auctions, and flea markets. They read and placed ads in the various trade papers. Of greatest significance, my father began to correspond daily with collectors around the world.

In the beginning stages of collecting, my father bought every item that was available. I think he feared that he would not see another. As he became more experienced he began to upgrade his collection so that it included only items in mint condition.

By 1972, his was the largest and most complete collection of serving trays in the country, and it included two one-of-a-kind trays.

It was at this point that my parents began cataloging trays with the Coca-Cola girls known as

Betty, Elaine, and Lillian. With the beautiful photographs and indexing completed, a book seemed a natural course. My parents introduced *Coca-Cola Collectibles, Volume I* in Indianapolis, Indiana, in 1972 at the first Advertising Antique Show. Because of the size and beauty of their collection, they were able to prepare a book each year after that. As the *Philadelphia Inquirer* of 1975 stated simply, "These books stimulated wider interest in collecting Coca-Cola items."

Photographs in this book were taken from these four volumes. Information about ordering can be found in the Source Directory.

17

Treasure hunting at swapmeets

If you are going to a swapmeet, go early. If you are a dealer with a booth, you usually have one hour to set up, so keep your display simple. As soon as you begin to unpack, you will find people roaming around to see what is around the next corner. Be ready. Much of the selling and trading is done before the doors ever open.

There is always a lot of activity at a swapmeet. Be careful about buying a questionable item. Use your book to identify the items and compare prices. Talk about your purchase with others; most dealers like to show their expertise.

There are always people who bring items to trade with the dealers. Sometimes they have an item that you have been wanting for a long time. This is a good chance to make a great swap.

Swapmeets are exciting and there are so many opportunities to meet new friends. Buy anything that suits your fancy. As long as it displays the familiar trademark, it is collectible.

Auctions—"Going once!"

Auctions are fast-paced and high energy! I have brought home some true finds from auctions. I have also bought things that I wouldn't normally buy and possibly paid too much for certain items on occasion.

There is always an auction preview. This is where bidders have a chance to view the merchandise and note the identification number of the items they intend to bid on later. Once the auctioneer begins, however, it's time to pay attention.

Someone will show the item while you take a good look. Depending on the type of auction, the auctioneer will either ask for a bid or possibly start the bidding himself. Whether you are holding a number or a card, any motion to the auctioneer signals a bid. Depending on the item, bidding will start low with six to ten people bidding back and forth. As the price increases, a few will quietly bow out of the bidding. It usually ends up with two people bidding back and forth until finally one no longer bids. "Two-hundred fifty, going once, going twice, $250 going three times. Sold for $250." To you? Maybe. If it seems a little frightening, start by bidding very low, as close to the original bid as possible. On the fourth of fifth bid, sit back and you will be outbid. At least this will give you some practice. If you want the item, bid for it. Don't forget that payment is required at the close of the auction.

Dating by slogans

An advertising slogan is the easiest way to date an item. Because of the amount of standardization in relation to the advertising, most ads had the same look and offered the same messages. During any specific year, an advertising slogan would appear in almost all mediums—blotters, billboards, signs, newspaper and magazine advertisements. The following is a list of the slogans used from 1900 to 1966, the approximate time period covered in this book.

1900
Deliciously refreshing
For headache and exhaustion, drink
   Coca-Cola

1904
Coca-Cola is a delightful, palatable,
   healthful beverage
Coca-Cola satisfies
Drink Coca-Cola in bottles—5¢

1905
Drink a bottle of carbonated Coca-Cola
Coca-Cola revives and sustains
Drink Coca-Cola at soda fountains
The favorite drink for ladies when
   thirsty, weary, and despondent
Good all the way down
Flows from every fountain
Sold in bottles

1906
The drink of quality
Thirst quenching—delicious and
   refreshing

1907
Delicious Coca-Cola, sustains, refreshes,
   invigorates
Cooling . . . refreshing . . . delicious
Coca-Cola is full of vim, vigor and go—
   is a snappy drink
Sold everywhere—5¢
Step into the nearest place and ask for a
   Coca-Cola
The great national drink

1908
Sparkling—harmless as water, and crisp
   as frost
The satisfactory beverage

1909
Delicious, wholesome, refreshing
Delicious, wholesome, thirst quenching
Drink delicious Coca-Cola
Whenever you see an arrow think of
   Coca-Cola

1910

Drink bottled Coca-Cola—so easily
served
It satisfies
Quenches the thirst as nothing else can

1911

It's time to drink Coca-Cola
Real satisfaction in every glass

1912

Demand the genuine—refuse substitutes

1913

Ask for it by its full name—then you will
get the genuine
The best beverage under the sun
It will satisfy you
A welcome addition to any party—
anytime—anywhere

1914

Demand the genuine by full name
Exhilarating, refreshing
Nicknames encourage substitutions
Pure and wholesome

1915

The standard beverage

1916

It's fun to be thirsty when you can get a
Coca-Cola
Just one glass will tell you

1917

Three million a day
The taste is the test of the Coca-Cola
quality
There's a delicious freshness to the
flavor of Coca-Cola

1919

Coca-Cola is a perfect answer to thirst
that no imitation can satisfy
It satisfies thirst
Quality tells the difference

1920

Drink Coca-Cola with soda
The hit that saves the day

1922

Quenching thirst everywhere
Thirst knows no season
Thirst can't be denied
Thirst reminds you—drink Coca-Cola

1923

Refresh yourself
A perfect blend of pure products from
nature
There's nothing like it when you're
thirsty

1924

Pause and refresh yourself

1925

The sociable drink
Stop at the red sign and refresh yourself

1926

Thirst and taste for Coca-Cola are the
same thing
Stop at the red sign

1927

Around the corner from anywhere
At the little red sign

1928

A pure drink of natural flavors

1929
The pause that refreshes

1930
Meet me at the soda fountain

1932
The drink that makes the pause
refreshing

1933
Don't wear a tired, thirsty face

1934
Carry a smile back to work
Ice-cold Coca-Cola is everywhere
else—it ought to be in your family
refrigerator
When it's hard to get started, start with a
Coca-Cola

1935
All trails lead to ice-cold Coca-Cola
The pause that brings friends together

1936
What refreshment ought to be
Get the feel of wholesome refreshment

1937
America's favorite moment
So easy to serve and so inexpensive
Stop for a pause . . . go refreshed

1938
Anytime is the right time to pause and
refresh
At the red cooler
The best friend thirst ever had
Pure sunlight

1939
Make lunch time refreshment time
Makes travel more pleasant
Thirst stops here

1940
The package that gets a welcome at home
Try it just once and you will know why

1941
A stop that belongs on your daily
timetable

1942
The only thing like Coca-Cola is Coca-
Cola itself
Refreshment that can't be duplicated

1943
That extra something
A taste all its own

1944
High sign of friendship
A moment on the sunnyside

1945
Whenever you hear "Have a Coke," you
hear the voice of America
Happy moment of hospitality
Coke means Coca-Cola

1947
Serving Coca-Cola serves hospitality
Relax with the pause that refreshes

1948
Where there's Coca-Cola there's
hospitality
Think of lunchtime as refreshment time

1949

Along the highway to anywhere

1950

Help yourself to refreshment

1951

Good food and Coca-Cola just naturally
  go together

1952

Coke follows thirst everywhere
The gift for thirst

1953

Dependable as sunrise

1954

For people on the go
Matchless flavor

1955

Almost everyone appreciates the best
America's preferred taste

1956

Feel the difference
Makes good things taste better

1957

Sign of good taste

1958

Refreshment the whole world prefers

1959

Cold, crisp taste that deeply satisfies
Make it a real meal

1960

Relax with Coke
Revive with Coke

1961

Coke and food—refreshing new feeling

1962

Enjoy that refreshing new feeling
Coca-Cola refreshes you best

1963

A chore's best friend
Things go better with Coke

1964

You'll go better refreshed

1965

Something more than a soft drink

1966

Coke . . . after Coke . . . after Coke

Grading condition

This guide to grading is the one established in 1965 by Sheldon Goldstein and has been unanimously used by collectors for almost three decades. Items can be classified and described in reference to their condition according to the following.

Special Rare Class. Items pre-1904 fall into this classification.

Mint. New condition. In original unused state. No visible marks.

Near-Mint. A classification into which most items that are thought of as mint would fall. Not in original mint condition. Close inspection would reveal very minor or slight marks of age or use.

Excellent. Only minor, hairline-type scratches visible without close examination. Small chip, chips, or marks on outer rim or edge of item.

Very Good. Minor surface scratch or scratches. Rust spots of no more than pinhead size. Minor flaking. Picture, lettering, and color in excellent condition.

Good. Minor scratch or scratches. Minor flaking. Minor facing. Possibly minor dents. Little rust or pitting.

Fair. Major scratch or scratches on surface. Picture or lettering faded. Rust spots on surface. Minor dent or dents. Bad chipping or flaking on surface.

Poor. Badly rusted, worn, dented, pitted, torn, Unrepairable.

Pricing

The most practical basis for pricing would seem to be what someone is willing to pay versus how much someone wants for an item. Without getting into the philosophy of sales, I can safely say that some Coke enthusiasts have no basis for what they are willing to pay.

Once while attending an auction, I talked with a woman who had been working on her Coca-Cola toy collection for years. She had been searching for five years when she finally found the 1938 toy stove. I feel the basis for her purchase must have been what she was willing and able to afford versus how much the dealer needed to sell his treasure.

In *The Classic Collector,* spring 1974, my father was quoted as saying, "When I first started collecting Coke items eight years ago, people were complaining that the prices were too high. Five years from now, today's prices will look cheap in comparison." When my father finally did sell his collection, his playing cards sold for $50 to $100 a pack. Today these cards have sold at auctions for as much as $500.

Coca-Cola collectibles
from A to Z

Blotters

Blotters were very popular in the first half of the century when dip pens and ink were used daily. Throughout the years, blotters have kept their basic oblong shape.

Slogan changes are significant as they depict the energy of the times. From 1927 to 1935, blotter artwork mimicked billboard artwork.

1-1. Set of six, 1920.

Many collectible blotters can be identified simply by the phrase written across the front.

1-2. "The Pause That Refreshes," 1930

1-3. "The Drink that keeps you feeling right," 1935

1-4. "Cold Refreshment," 1937

1-5. "Anytime is the right time to pause and refresh," 1938

1-6. "The Drink everybody knows," 1939

1-7. "Bring in your thirst and go away without it," 1940

1-8. "Completely refreshing," 1941

1-9. "Refreshment that can't be duplicated," 1942

1-10. "A Taste all its own," 1943

1-11. "How about a Coke," 1944

1-12. "Passport to Refreshment," 1945

1-13. "Coke knows no season," 1947

1-14. "Delicious and Refreshing," 1951

1-15. "Friendliest Drink on Earth," 1956

1-16. Blotter, 1904.

1-17. Blotter, 1928.

1-18. Blotter, 1929.

1-19. Blotter, 1947.

Bookmarks

Many Coca-Cola bookmarks are still in existence. People who are collecting books are frequently finding Coke bookmarks between the pages.

2-2. Hilda Clark, 1899.

2-1. Hilda Clark, 1900.

2-3. Hilda Clark, 1902.

2-4. Lillian Nordica, 1903, 6″ × 2″.

2-6. Lillian Russell, 1904.

2-5. Coca-Cola Chewing Gum,
2″ × 6″, 1908.

2-7. Owl, 1906.

Books

3-1. *The Romance of Coca-Cola,* 1916. Describes the history of Coca-Cola through 1916.

3-3. *Alphabet Book of Coca-Cola,* 1928.

3-2. *Facts,* 1923.

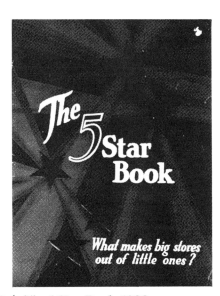

3-4. *The 5 Star Book,* 1928.

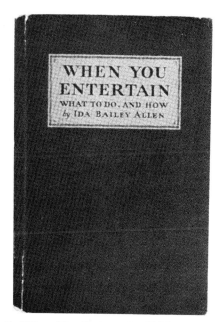

3-5. *When You Entertain,* 1932.

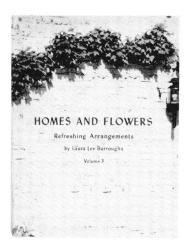

3-7. *Home and Flowers,* 1940, by Laura Burroughs.

3-8. *A Fascinating Hobby, Flower Arranging,* 1940.

3-6. *The Red Barrel,* 1940. These books, which were given to U.S. soldiers, kept our fighting men and women current of important news events.

3-9. *My Daily Reminder,* 1939.

3-10. *Know your War Planes,* 1943.

3-12. *Our America,* 1946. These books were distributed to schools.

3-11. *The Coca-Cola Bottler,* 1944.

3-13. *Easy Hospitality,* 1957.

3-14. *Pause for Living,* 1961.

3-16. Paper writing pad, 1960.

3-15. Paper writing pad, 1950.

3-17. *Flags of the United Nations,* 1960.

Bottles

Here's how Coke bottles evolved over the years.

Hutchinson bottle, 1894, was the first bottle used by the Biedenharn Candy Company

Hutchinson bottle, 1899 to 1902, first bottle to be marked with the Coca-Cola script

Straight-sided bottle, 1900 to 1916,
the first bottle to use the crown cork closure

Hobble skirt, 1915, designed by the Root Glass company

Christmas bottle, 1923, the first universal design, was patented December 25, 1923

33

Christmas bottle, 1937, standardized in 1948 to hold 6¹/₂ ounces

ACL bottle, 1957, introduced the first applied color label

No return bottle, 1961, was the first one-way glass bottle. It was later modified to include a twist cap

Plastic bottle, 1975, is an experimental plastic bottle tested from 1970 to 1975

4-1. Biedenharn Candy Company, 1894.

| 1894 | 1899–1902 | 1900 ----- 1916 | 1915 Nov. 16 | 1923 Dec. 25 | 1937 Aug. 3 (D-105529) | 1957 Applied Color Label (ACL) | 1961 One-Way Bottle (OWB) | 1975 One-Way Bottle (Plastic) |

Chronology of the glass package for Coca-Cola 1894-1975.

4-2. Biedenharn bottle, 1900.

4-4. Hutchinson bottle, 1902.

4-3. Biedenharn candy, 1900.

4-5. Syrup bottle, 1910. These bottles were given to drugstores for storing syrup to be mixed with seltzer.

4-6. Coca-Cola syrup bottle, 1910.

4-8. Coca-Cola syrup bottle, 1920.

4-7. Drink Coca-Cola syrup bottle, 1910.

4-9. Drink Coca-Cola syrup bottle, 1920.

4-10. Christmas display bottle, 20″, 1923. These bottles were full when on display.

4-12. Experimental plastic bottle, 1974. Some of these are still found full.

4-11. Hutchinson commemorative, 1961.

4-13. Syrup jug, 1930. Syrup was also delivered in barrels.

37

Older bottles can be dated fairly easily if you look for the series of manufacturer's numbers on the base or on the bottom of the bottle. For the number 18-30, for example, the first two digits (18) indicate the mold number. The second two (30) indicate the year of manufacture.

Presently, Coca-Cola bottlers code the four numbers somewhat differently. The first digit indicates the year; the second, the mold; the third, the manufacturer's symbol; and the fourth digit, the glass plant.

Another possibility for identification is bottle weight. The empty weights for Coca-Cola bottles get lighter each year (see the chart below).

Date	Empty weight ounces
1916 to 1936	14.24
1937 to 1956	14.01
1957 to 1958	13.80
1958 to 1962	13.65
1966 to present	13.26

Calendars

The first Coca-Cola calendar was issued in 1891. The first ten years displayed wholesome and pretty, but anonymous girls. As the company grew, they were able to engage the desirable actress Hilda Clark and the celebrated Metropolitan Opera star, Lillian Nordica, as models. After 1920, most calendars were released once again with unnamed models.

Many were printed in two versions, one with the model holding a Coke glass, the other, a Coke bottle. Since these calendars were distributed by bottlers, there are more calendars displaying bottles than glasses. Calendars with both renditions came out in the following years: 1903, 1904, 1914, 1915, 1916, 1917, 1919, 1920, 1923, and 1927.

It is very difficult to find a calendar complete with pad or all calendar pages intact. Without pad or pages, calendars cannot be considered in mint condition. They are still very beautiful and valuable, however.

5-1. The first Coca-Cola calendar printed by Calvert Lithography Company of Atlanta, Georgia, 1891.

5-3. Calendar illustration without the pad, 1898.

5-2. This calendar shows the first coupon offering a free Coca-Cola, 1897.

5-4. In the same condition as the 1898 issue, 1899.

5-5. Calendar for 1901.

5-7. The model in this 1903 calendar holds the same glassholder used in the 1902 issue. Both calendars were printed by the same company.

5-6. This photograph of Hilda Clark for the 1902 calendar was copyrighted in 1900 by Morrison of Chicago. The printing was done by Wolf and Company, Philadelphia.

5-8. Lillian Nordica decorates both this 1904 issue and the 1905 version. This same calendar photograph exists elsewhere with one change—instead of the glass on the table, there is a bottle.

5-11. Good to the Last Drop, 1908 issue. Maxwell House later made this slogan famous with their coffee.

5-9. Calendar for 1906.

5-10. Calendar for 1907.

5-12. This 1909 calendar has the same photograph of Lillian Nordica that was used on the 1905 issue.

5-13. This 1910 issue is a "top" only.

5-15. This calendar, issued in 1912, is the first featuring two models.

5-14. Coca-Cola girl calendar for 1910.

5-16. Calendar for 1913.

5-17. Betty was one of the most popular Coca-Cola girls ever. She appears on almost all of the advertising pieces of 1914, including this calendar. In 1970, a Betty calendar could be found for $100.

5-19. The Knitting Girl, 1916.

5-18. This 1915 calendar's value increases $300 if the model is pictured holding a bottle.

5-20. World War I Girl, 1917.

5-21. Also issued in 1917.

5-23. Calendar for 1919.

5-22. Calendar for 1918.

5-24. The Garden Girl, 1920.

5-25. Calendar for 1921.

5-27. Calendar for 1923.

5-26. The Autumn Girl, 1922.

5-28. Calendar for 1924.

5-29. Calendar for 1925.

5-31. Calendar for 1926.

5-30. Calendar for 1927.

5-32. Calendar for 1928.

5-34. The Bathing Beauty, 1930.

5-33. Calendar for 1929.

5-35. Farm Boy with Dog, painted by Norman Rockwell for 1931 issue, often called "Tom Sawyer" by collectors.

47

5-36. Norman Rockwell 1932 calendar, affectionately referred to as "Huckleberry Finn."

5-38. A Norman Rockwell 1934 issue.

5-37. The Village Blacksmith by Frederic Stanley, 1933 issue.

5-39. Norman Rockwell, 1935 issue.

5-40. Artist N. C. Wyeth produced this 1936 issue.

5-41. N. C. Wyeth, 1937 issue.

5-42. Created by Bradshaw Crandall, 1938.

5-43. Notice that the glass in the photograph for this calendar is unmarked, 1939.

Calendars dated before 1940 are much harder to find. Luckily, Coca-Cola continued the practice of calendar advertising during the war years. Less expensive and more easily obtainable, the following calendars are very collectible.

Cars and trucks

6-2. Drink Coca-Cola in bottles, 1945.

6-1. Sprite Boy, 1945.

6-3. Coke truck, 1950.

6-7. Buddy L truck, 1960.

6-4. Open truck, 1950.

6-8. Coke can car, 1972.

6-5. Car, 1950.

6-9. Semi truck, 1972.

6-6. Bus, 1950.

6-10. Truck, 1973.

Cars and trucks not illustrated include:

6-11. Metalcraft truck, 1930, 11″ rubber wheels.

6-12. Metalcraft truck, 1930, with working headlights.

6-13. Budgie truck, 5″, yellow, 1950s.

6-14. Early matchbook truck, 2¼″, 1950s.

6-15. Enclosed truck, 1950s.

6-16. Ford station wagon, 5″, 1950s.

6-17. Marx truck, 1950s, cases and bottles.

6-18. Marx truck, 1950s, cases, bottles, miniature hand truck.

6-19. Marx truck, plastic, 1950s, Louis Marx & Company, New York.

6-20. Truck, 8″, 1950s.

6-21. Bottle truck, 4½″, semi, 1960s.

6-22. Buddy L, 1960s.

6-23. Pickup, 1960s.

6-24. Things Go Better with Coke, 4½″, 1960s.

6-25. Truck, 2¾″, 1960s.

6-26. Flatbed, 1½″, 1970.

6-27. Roadster model, 1971.

6-28. Eight-wheeler truck, 9½″, 1974.

6-29. Modern logo truck, 1974.

6-30. Bus, double-decker, 3″, 1975.

Cartons and bottle holders

7-1. Shipping case, 1906.

7-2. Six-bottle holder, 1933.

7-3. July Fourth wrapper, 1935.

7-5. Six-bottle holder, 1937.

7-4. Take-home carton, 1939.

53

7-6. Take-home cartons, 1940.

7-7. Car window holder, 1940.

7-8. Car bottle holder, 1950.

Clocks

Baird Clock Company produced the first clock used to promote the Coca-Cola Company. Soda fountains that sold over one-hundred gallons a year were able to obtain a clock. The advertisement was embossed on the circular plaster of Paris frame.

The company later standardized their advertising message and promoted "Drink Coca-Cola" on all clocks.

The Gilbert Clocks from the 1920s have become easier to obtain. They are also easy to identify. Look for the sticker glued to the back, which states: "The Wm. L. Gilbert Clock Co., Winsted, Conn."

8-2. Baird clock, 1893.

8-1. Baird clock, very rare, 1892.

8-3. Desk clock, embossed bottles, 1907.

8-4. Desk clock, 1907.

8-6. Dome clock, 1910.

8-5. Drink Coca-Cola, 40″ × 18″, 1909.

8-7. Wall clock, 1915.

8-8. Pocket watch, 1920.

8-10. Reissue clock, 1972.

8-9. Dome clock, two bottles, 1950.

8-11. Reissue Betty clock, 1974.

Coca-Cola chewing gum

While most people associate the familiar Coca-Cola trademark with the popular soda, the logo also has been used to represent other items. In 1908, the Franklin Manufacturing Company of Richmond, Virginia, produced a chicle that "aids digestion and gives comfort after a hearty meal."

Coca-Cola Pepsin Gum was introduced in a catalog by Schaack & Sons of Chicago. Twenty packages, five cents each, sold wholesale for sixty cents.

The glass Coca-Cola Chewing Gum roulette wheel shown on page 60 was displayed for many years on a drugstore counter in a small town in South Carolina. It is the size of a dinner plate and weighs three or four pounds. A marble rolls around the interior circumference of the wheel and drops into one of the numbered slots in the center. Children probably used the roulette wheel to win either a stick of gum or possibly a glass of Coke.

In 1980, an antiques store merchant from South Carolina wrote after reading my monthly column in the *American Collector.* He had acquired this piece twenty years earlier when he purchased the estate of the woman who had once owned the above mentioned drugstore. He kept the roulette wheel for many years on his own counter. Although he had never intended to sell it, he explained that he needed money to put his son through college. He offered to sell it to me.

This roulette wheel has the second highest value of any chewing gum-related item. Because it is one-of-a-kind, I am very proud to have it in my collection.

My father discovered the very rare 1902 cylindrical gum dispenser illustrated here from a man who collected only chewing gum dispensers. When my father later sold it to the Schmidt Museum, this one-of-a-kind collectible brought top dollar.

9-1. Coca-Cola Gum, 1902.

9-2. Cylindrical gum dispenser, 1902.

9-3. Ad in *Everybody's Magazine,* 1904.
9-4. Similar ad in *Everybody's Magazine,* 1906.

9-6. Bookmark, 1904, "The Gum That's Pure Contains The Tonic Properties of Coca-Cola and Pure Pepsin." A book dealer ran across this very rare item in a book.

9-5. Gum package wrapper, 1906, Manufactured by the Franklin Caro Co.

9-7. Shipping case, 1906.

59

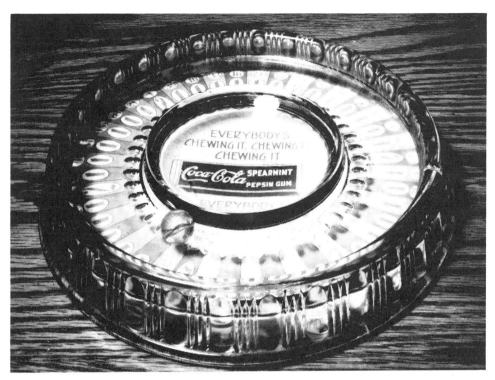

9-8. Glass roulette wheel, 1908.

9-9. Coca-Cola Gum fan, 1910, front and
back. The front of the fan shows the
Franklin Caro Manufacturing Company,
Richmond, Virginia.

9-10. Gum display box, 1913.

9-11. Gum display shipping box, 1913. Placed in plastic for preservation.

9-13. Apothecary jars, 1915. Coca-Cola Pepsin Gum. 9-14. Coca-Cola Chewing Gum.

9-12. Coca-Cola Gum paperweight, 1916.

Coolers and miniatures

10-1. Embossed bottles and cases, 1920. The bottles are glass.

10-3. Salesman's sample cooler, 10″ × 11″, 1934.

10-4. Salesman's sample cooler, 10″ × 11″, 1934.

10-2. Miniature glass perfume bottle, 1930.

10-5. Bottle ice cooler, 1934. Held block ice to cool bottles.

10-6. Plastic dispenser, 1950.

10-8. Miniature plastic bottle, 1951.

10-7. Miniature bottle lighter, 1950.

10-9. Plastic dispenser, 1960.

10-10. Plastic bottles and case, 1971.

10-13. Miniature six pack, 1973.

10-11. King and regular size bottles and case, 1971.

10-14. Miniature six pack, gold metal, 1973.

10-12. Plastic bottles and case, 1973.

Coupons

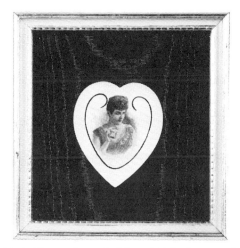

11-1. Heart-shaped, 2″ × 2¹/₄″, front and back, 1898.

11-2. Celluloid, 1899.

11-3. Hilda Clark, 3³/₄″ × 1¹/₂″, front and back, 1900.

11-4. Lillian Russell, 1904.

11-6. Delicious and Refreshing, 1904.

11-5. Three coupons, 1905, each.

11-7. Coupon book, 1920.

11-9. Golfer, 1928.

11-8. Soda jerk, 1927.

11-10. Take Home a Carton, 1939.

Fans

These fans were given to stores and distributed to the customers.

12-1. Drive with Care, 1928.

12-2. Quality Carries On, 1942.

12-3. Drink Coca-Cola, 1950.

Glass items and lamps

13-1. Syrup dispenser, 1895. The syrup has saturated the porous ceramic.

13-2. Glass change receiver, Hilda Clark, 1900.

13-3. Ceramic change receiver, 1900, made by Charles Lippincott & Company of Philadelphia.

13-6. Milk glass shade, 1920.

13-7. Glass change receiver, 7″ dia., 1920, made by Wolf & Company, Lithographers.

13-4. Leaded glass bottle, 36″ high, 1920.

13-5. Milk glass light fixture, 1920, marked on top band—"Property of the Coca-Cola Company. To be returned upon demand."

13-8. Snack bowl, 1920.

13-9. Leaded glass globe, 1928.

13-10. Lenox china plate, 10$\frac{1}{2}$″ dia., 1950.

13-11. World dish, 11$\frac{1}{2}$″ × 11$\frac{1}{2}$″, 1967. Shows where Coca-Cola is sold around the world.

13-12. China plate, 10$\frac{1}{2}$″ dia., 1930.

13-13. World dish, 7½″ dia., 1967.

13-14. Swedish glass plate, 8¼″ × 6¼″, 1969. Originally came in a felt bag.

Glasses

14-1. Coca-Cola 5¢, 1900.

14-2. Drink Coca-Cola, 1905.

14-3. Pewter, 1930.

14-4. Coca-Cola, 1935.

Knives

15-1. Knife and corkscrew, brass, 1906, both sides shown.

15-2. Switchblade, bone handle, 1908.

15-3. Compliments the Coca-Cola Co., 1930.

15-4. One blade, 1930.

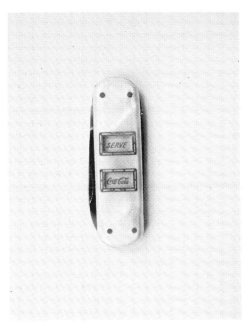

15-5. Serve Coca-Cola, 1950.

Magazine advertising

Early advertising showed elaborately dressed people drinking Coca-Cola. The slogans always emphasized the popular Coca-Cola trademark. Advertisements for Coke appeared frequently in these publications: *The Housekeeper, Woman's Home Companion, Ladies' Home Journal, Redbook, Better Homes and Gardens, McCall's, Sports Illustrated, National Geographic, Motor Trend, Car Craft, Sports Car Graphic, Hot Rod, Boys Life, American Girl, Seventeen, Saturday Evening Post, Success, Literary Digest, Life, Delineator, Sunset, Pictorial Review,* and *Farm and Home.*

Two-color ads appeared on both the front and back covers of these publications: *The Housewife, The Household,* and *People's Popular Monthly.*

Miscellaneous

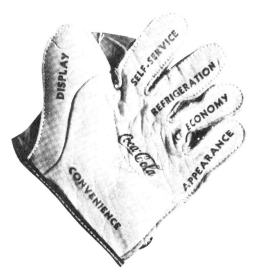

16-1. Baseball glove, 1927.

16-3. Comb, 1940.

16-4. Cowboy hat, 1974.

16-2. Car key, 1950.

16-5. Doorknob, 1920. Purchased from a man who bought some doors at an old hotel.

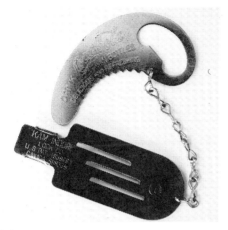

16-6. Door lock, 1910. "Kam-Indore Lock Co.," also bottle opener.

16-7. Door push (porcelain), 1930. Placed across the screen door at grocery stores so that customers couldn't put their hands through the screen.

16-9. "A Float with a Coke" (plastic), 1945, container holds ice cream.

16-8. Door push, 1950, very popular.

16-10. Fountain seat, 1910.

16-11. Golf tee set, 1950.

16-14. License plate, 1950. Background is white with red lettering.

16-15. License plate, 1950. Red background with white lettering.

16-12. Keychain, 1955.

16-13. Kit Carson poster, 1950.

16-16. Krumkake maker, 1920.

16-17. Magic lantern pictures, "Stop at the Red Sign," 1926. This and other similar hand-painted glass slides were used as commercials during intermission. Produced in St. Louis for one dollar. Other signs include "A Home Run," 1927, 16-18; "Good Company!" 16-19; and "Unanimous Good Taste," 1928, 16-20.

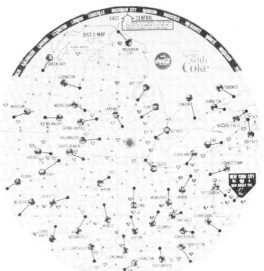

16-21. Needle case, 1924.

16-23. Mileage table, cardboard, 1950.

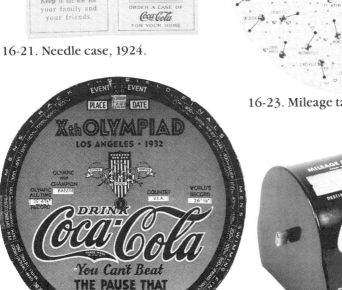

16-22. Olympic record indicator, 1932. Souvenirs from the 1932 Olympics. Coca-Cola was a sponsor at the tenth games.

16-24. Mileage and route information indicator, bright red, 1950. Gives distance from one location to another.

16-27. Set of place mats, 1974.

16-25. Pillow, 1940.

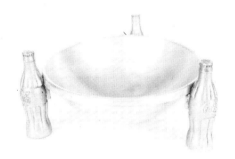

16-28. Pretzel dish, aluminum, 1936.

16-26. Perfume bottle and holder, sterling silver, 1924. Inscribed "Top Hat Jewelry by Wells." The top flips open to the side and holds the dauber in place.

16-29. Safety marker, 1900. Used at crosswalks.

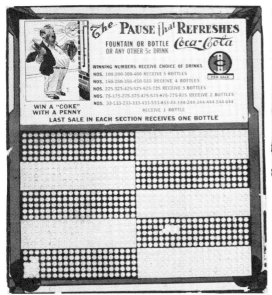

16-32. U.S. Navy sewing kit, 1941.

16-30. Punchboards, 1929 (same price for the 1920 issue). People bought punches hoping to win three five-cent bottles of Coke.

16-33. Sugar rationing book, 1943.

16-31. Salt and pepper shakers, 1920.

16-34. Token, 1930. A giveaway used as a slug to obtain a free Coke from a machine.

16-35. Thimble, aluminum, 1920.

16-48. Planter sconce, 1920.

16-36. Token holder, 1943. Used to hold O.P.A. rationing tokens.

Other items not pictured, but equally collectible, include:

16-37. Binoculars, 1910.
16-38. Celluloid pencil holder, 1910.
16-39. Wooden bench, 1910, "Coca-Cola in bottles" written across the backrest.
16-40. Commemorative fifty-dollar gold coin, 1915.
16-41. Convention pin, 1916.
16-42. Silverware, 1920.
16-43. Driver's hat pin, 1930.
16-44. Pencil box, 1930.
16-45. Pencil sharpener, 1933.

16-46. First aid kit, 1940.
16-47. Ice pick and opener, 1940.
16-49. U.S. Army sewing kit, 1941.
16-50. Baseball bat, 1950.
16-51. Kit Carson handkerchief, 1950.
16-52. Pen, 1950.
16-53. Bottle cap sharpener, 1960.
16-54. Hall of Fame records, 1960.
16-55. Pledge pin.
16-56. Five-year.
16-57. Ten-year.
16-58. Fifteen-year.
16-59. Twenty-year.
16-60. Thirty-year.
16-61. Fifty-year.

Newspaper advertising

The first newspaper advertisements were most often placed by individual bottlers. In 1906, the D'Arcy agency began standardizing advertising copy. Coca-Cola made many appeals to their distributors for uniformity. In 1926, just over one-half of all bottlers were using company-prepared advertisements.

In 1939, the Coca-Cola Company offered their bottlers a cooperative advertising program. Based on per capita consumption, the company assumed from 50 to 80 percent of all advertising costs. They also provided art for ads that bottlers could place in their local newspapers. For obvious reasons, this lessened the amount of individually created advertisements.

Newspaper advertisements are a pictorial representation of the history of both the Coca-Cola Company and the United States. A chronological collection of these slogans makes a very nice collection.

Openers

17-3. Opener, 1910.

17-1. Bone-handled knife, 1908.

17-2. Spoon opener.

17-4. Opener, 1920.

17-5. Fiftieth anniversary, 1952.

17-7. Boot knife opener. From a private collection of knives.

17-6. Coca-Cola in sterilized bottles.

17-8. Have a Coke.

17-9. Block print opener.

17-13. Flat-shaped bottle opener.

17-10. Oval-shaped bottle opener.

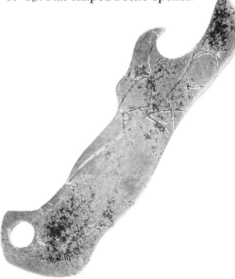

17-11. Skate key opener.

17-14. Legs opener.

17-12. Drink Coca-Cola.

17-15. Beer-type opener.

17-16. Coca-Cola in bottles.

18-2. Hilda Clark note pad, 1902.

Paper items

18-1. Celluloid postage stamp holder, 1901. Stamps go in between the pages so they don't stick together.

18-3. Celluloid note pad, 1902.

18-6. Opera program, 1906.

18-4. Trade card, folded and unfolded, 1905. Distributed by Western Coca-Cola Bottling.

18-7. Pocket secretary, 1920. Given to management within the bottling companies. There is a pen inside.

18-8. Book cover, 1925. Distributed to school bookstores to be given to book purchasers.

18-5. Note pad, 1905.

18-9. Nature study cards, 1928.

18-12. Bottle bags, 1932.

18-10. Miniature ad, 1929.

18-11. Souvenir money, 1931. Confederate one-hundred dollar bill.

18-13. Score pad, 1941.

18-14. Plant tour gift, 1948.

18-15. Cards, 1943, produced during a time when schools were having regular air raid drills. These were provided to schools to help teach children how to spot enemy planes.

18-16. Book cover, 1951.

Playing cards

19-1. Coca-Cola Relieves Fatigue girl, straight-sided bottle and straw, blue inset border, 1909, copyright by S. L. Whitten, Chicago, Illinois.

19-2. Girl with a Parasol, 1915. Western Coca-Cola Bottling Company of Chicago, Illinois, offered these cars for twenty-five cents in stamps. The joker shows a straight-sided bottle with a paper label.

19-5. The Ice Skater, 1956. Commemorates the seventieth anniversary of Coca-Cola.

19-3. Girl with Bobbed Hair . . . Tastes Good, 1928. These cards have four different borders: red, light yellow, light gray, and red with gold edge.

19-6. The Girl with a Bowling Ball, 1961.

19-4. The Stewardess, 1943. During the war Coca-Cola distributed the double-deck bridge sets depicting the nurse and the switchboard operator. They sold for thirty-three cents to the bottlers.

19-7. Boy and Girl at Fireplace, 1963.

Additional sets not pictured include:

19-8. Hund and Egler Bottling Company, 1937–1939.
19-9. The Party, 1951.
19-10. Sign of Good Taste, 1959.
19-11. Be Really Refreshed, 1960.
19-12. Coke Refreshes You Best, 1961.
19-13. Things Go Better with Coke, 1963.
19-14. Zing! Refreshing New Feeling, 1963.
19-15. It's the Real Thing, 1971.
19-16. Drink Coca-Cola, 1974.
19-17. Coca-Cola Adds Life to Everything, 1976.
19-18. Enjoy Coca-Cola, 1976.

Pocket mirrors

Women frequently carried pocket mirrors because they could be stored conveniently in their purses. There are many reproductions, but they are easy to spot once you've seen an original.

Information shown in quotation marks is the copy as written on the bottom and side rim of the mirror. This is the easiest way to identify an original. Before 1913, all pocket mirrors came with the following copy: "Duplicate Mirrors 5¢ Postage, Coca-Cola Company, Atlanta, Ga."

20-1. Oval, "Bastian Bros. Co. Rochester, N.Y.," 1903.

20-2. St. Louis, "J.B. Carroll Chicago," 1904.

20-3. Juanita, "The Whitehead & Hoag Co., Newark, N.J.," 1905.

20-5. Coca-Cola girl, "J.B. Carroll Chicago," 1909.

20-4. Relieves Fatigue, "From the Painting Copyright 1906, by Wolf & Co. Phila. Bastian Bros. Co. Roch. N.Y.," 1906.

20-6. Coca-Cola girl, "The Whitehead & Hoag Co. Newark, N.J.," 1911.

20-7. Oval, 1914.

20-9. Bathing suit girl, "The Whitehead & Hoag Co. Newark, N.J.," 1918. The hardest to find, only three are known to exist.

20-8. Elaine, "The Whitehead & Hoag Co. Newark, N.J.," 1917.

20-10. Garden girl, "Bastian Bros. Co. Rochester, N.Y.," 1920.

Postcards

21-1. Duster girl, 5¹/₂″ × 3¹/₂″, 1906.

Other postcards not illustrated:

21-3. Delivery wagon, 1900.
21-4. Bottling plant, 1904.
21-5. Bottling plant, 1905.
21-6. Bottling plant, 1906.
21-7. Bottling plant, 1910.

21-8. Delivery wagon, 1913.

21-2. The Coca-Cola girl, 5¹/₂″ × 3¹/₂″, 1909.

21-9. Delivery wagon, 1915.

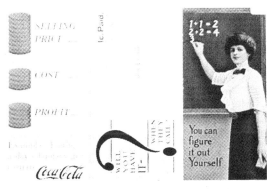

ALL OVER THE WORLD

You will find *Coca-Cola* signs that create a demand which you must supply. Don't miss the chance.

It's the sign of prosperity

21-10. All Over The World, 1913.

21-11. Foldout, 1913. This postcard came in five versions.

21-12. Dick Tracy, 1942.

Radio advertising

Many of Coca-Cola's first radio spots were recorded on disks that are widely traded and collected.

The Coca-Cola Company began its radio advertising in 1927 with a fourteen-week program about the romance between Vivian, the first Coca-Cola girl, and the public, personified as Jim.

In 1930, Coca-Cola began sponsoring a radio show that featured celebrity hosts. This show was expanded in 1934 and 1935. Complete with a sixty-five piece orchestra and a twenty-five member vocal group, "The Pause That Refreshes" was a half-hour of popular music with three Coca-Cola advertisements.

Until the advent of television in the early 1950s, the Coca-Cola Company sponsored a wide variety of radio programs. One memorable show began in November of 1941 and was called "Spotlight Bands." The show featured a series of different bands selected to entertain young Americans in the Armed Forces.

Other programs featured such radio and music stars as Percy Faith, Spike Jones, Edgar Bergen and Charlie McCarthy, and Mario Lanza. Although Coca-Cola began to focus more on television advertising in the 1950s, it had its greatest radio hit in 1970 with a song called, "I'd Like to Buy the World a Coke." The song was so successful that Coca-Cola revised it and changed the title to, "I'd Like to Teach the World to Sing." The two versions sold over one million copies with all the proceeds going to UNICEF.

Because there are people who save only old radio serials, it is possible to find and own a nice collection of Coca-Cola broadcasts.

Radios

Coca-Cola didn't use radios for advertising until the 1930s. The radios always resemble either a cooler, bottle, or can.

22-1. Bottle radio, 1930.

22-2. Cooler radio, 1949.

22-3. Crystal radio, 1950.

22-4. Transistor, 7$^1/_2$″ × 3$^1/_2$″, 1963.

22-6. Coke can radio, 1971.

22-5. Transistor, 4$^1/_2$″ × 2$^1/_2$″, 1963.

22-7. Transistor, 1972.

Records and music

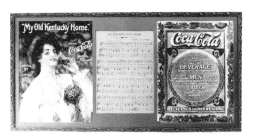

23-1. Sheet music, 13½″ × 10½″, 1905, set.

23-2. A similar set including "Old Folks at Home," "Juanita," "Lead Kindly Light," and "Nearer, My God to Thee" was found in a piano bench recently when an estate was settled.

23-3. Sheet music, 8″ × 10½″, 1928.

23-4. Morton Downey record, 1940. Famous radio singer.

23-5. Training record, 16″ dia., 1945. Used for training employees.

23-6. Tony Bennett record, 1951.

continued on page 105

1. Lillian Russell oilcloth, 25″ × 44″, 1904.

2. Hilda Clark, tin, 20″ × 28″, 1900.

3. Cameo mirror, 6′ × 4′, 1905.

4. Leaded glass, Tiffany-style chandelier,
22″ × 11″ × 7½″, 1910.

5. Cylindrical gum, 1902.

6. Oval change tray, $4^3/8'' \times 6^1/8''$,
   "Coca-Cola Girl," 1909.

7. Oval change tray, $4^3/8'' \times 6^1/8''$,
   1912.

8. Cigar band, 1927.

9. Metalcraft truck, 11″ long, 1930.
10. With working headlights.

11. Buddy Lee doll,
     12 ¹/₂″ tall, 1928.

12. Santa Claus, 1940.

13. Salesman's sample cooler, 1934.

Records and music (continued)

Sheet music, 1971. cover.

23-8. "It's the Real Thing," 1971.

23-7. Sheet music, 1971.

23-9. Sheet music, 1969.

23-10. Record series, 1971: "The Lone Ranger," "Superman," "Sgt. Preston of The Yukon," and "Dick Tracy." These are the actual old radio shows that were part of the afternoon series. Coca-Cola advertisements appear on the backs of the albums.

23-11. W. C. Fields record, 1971. Part of the same afternoon series. This particular album is more valuable because of the girls photographed on the front.

106

St. Nicholas and Coke

The bishop of Myra lived in the country of Lycia in Asia Minor around 300 A.D. It was this man with the gentle nature and dedication to children and mankind that the legend of St. Nicholas is based on.

In 1882, Clement Clarke Moore's poem "Twas the Night Before Christmas," promoted St. Nicholas' image as that of a pixie-like character.

The image of Santa Claus changed over the years. By 1931, the artist Haddon Sundblom had developed a realistic portrait of Santa Claus that would be used in Christmas advertisements for years to come.

Some characteristics of Haddon's Santa were white hair and a long beard, a long red coat trimmed in white fur, a leather belt with a buckle, and high boots.

Santa Claus memorabilia can make a very fascinating collection. The following slogans connected Santa and Coca-Cola on cards, billboards, magazine advertisements, blotters, etc.

"The Busiest Man in the World comes up smiling after . . . the pause that refreshes," 1930 (this was the first Coke advertisement with Santa Claus in it)

"Please Pause Here, Jimmy," 1932

"Away with a tired thirsty face. Bounce back to normal," 1933 (shows Santa taking off a tired yawning face)

"The pause that keeps you going," 1934

"It will refresh you too," 1935

"Me too. The pause that refreshes," 1936

"Give and take, say I," 1937 (shows Santa drinking a bottle of Coke and eating a piece of chicken from someone's refrigerator)

"Thanks for the pause that refreshes," 1938

"And the same to you," 1939

"Somebody knew I was coming," 1940

"Thirst asks nothing more" 1941
"Drink Coca-Cola," 1943
"Here's to G.I. Joes," 1944 (Sprite and Santa)
"They knew what I wanted," 1945
"For me," 1946
"Busy man's pause," 1947
"Hospitality," 1948
"For Santa," 1950
"Now it's my time," 1951
"Almost everyone appreciates the best," 1955
"Twas the Coke before Christmas," 1956
"Santa's pause," 1958 (shows Santa taking off his boots)

After 1960, Santa advertisements included popular slogans such as "Things go better with Coke."

Signs

24-1. Bottle tray, 20″ × 10¹/₈″, 1900.

24-2. Celluloid bottle sign, 1900.

24-3. Hilda Clark, tin, 20″ × 28″, 1899.

24-4. Hilda Clark, paper, 15″ × 20″, 1900.

24-5. Lillian Nordica, oval, 8¼″ × 10¼″, 1903.

24-7. Lillian Nordica, cardboard, 25″ × 39″, 1904.

24-6. Betty, tin, 30″ × 40″, 1914.

24-8. Elaine, tin, 20″ × 30″, 1917.

24-9. St. Louis Fair, cardboard,
28″ × 44″, 1904.

24-10. Cameo matte poster, 1904.

24-11. Tin, 27″ × 19″, 1907.

24-12. Coca-Cola in bottles, chrome 1920.

24-14. Cherub, 1908.

24-15. Stand-up version with easel back (rare).

24-16. Arrow, tin, 30″ × 7³/₄″, 1927.

24-13. Bottle, tin, 3′, 1923.

24-17. Coca-Cola girls, cardboard, 1922.

24-18. Tin sign, 13″ × 6″, 1931.

24-20. Wooden sign, dated 1935.

24-21. Plastic sign, 9″ diameter, c. 1940.

24-19. Porcelain sign, dated 1950.

Other signs not pictured include:

24-22. Cardboard die-cut, 1912, 18″ × 21″.

24-23. Paper signs, 1920, 12″ × 20″ Delicious and Refreshing.

24-24. Pause a Minute—Refresh Yourself.

24-25. That Taste Good Feeling.

24-26. Treat Yourself Right.

24-27. An Ice Cold with a Red Hot.

24-28. Off to a Fresh Start.

24-29. It's Delicious, cardboard, 9″ × 12″, 1930.

Cut-out window displays, 1932.

24-30. Joan Blondell.

24-31. Sue Carol.

24-32. Jean Harlow.

24-33. Lupe Velez.

24-34. Paper sign, 1932, 11″ × 21½″, Lupe Velez.

24-35. Wallace Beery, cardboard, 14″ × 29″, 1934.

24-36. Wallace Beery and Jackie Cooper, 1934, 4½ foot-long window display piece.

Cardboard, 14″ × 30″, 1936.

24-37. Ice Cold.

24-38. It Cools You.

24-39. Refreshing.

Large cardboard signs, 29″ × 50″.

24-40. 50th Anniversary, 1936.

24-41. "For people on the go," 1940.

24-42. "He's coming home tomorrow," 1940s.

24-43. Home-Refreshment, 1940s.

24-44. The year-round answer to thirst, 1941.

24-45. Refreshment Right out of the Bottle, 1942.

Superstar cardboard signs, 11″ × 14″, 1950s.

24-46. Roy Campanella, Sugar Ray Robinson, Monte Irvin, Bill Bruton, Larry Doby, Satchel Paige, and Lionel Hampton.

Festoons

Festoons, collectible but not shown, are:

25-1. Coca-Cola girls, 1927.

25-2. Coca-Cola girls, 1951.

25-3. Coca-Cola girls, 1958.

Backbar displays

25-4. Antique cars, 1950.

25-5. Square dance, 1950.

25-6. State tree, 1950.

25-7. Girls' heads, 1951.

Festoons connected by ribbons

25-8. Cornflower.

25-9. Hollyhock.

25-10. Morning glory.

25-11. Verbena.

Smoking paraphernalia

Match safes and holders were useful and elegant for carrying wooden matches; however, they were expensive to manufacture. Later, paper matches were produced easily and inexpensively. However, they were less durable and therefore are more difficult to find.

Matchbooks not pictured include:

26-1. Ask for a Bottle, 1908.
26-4. Drink Coca-Cola in Bottles, 1912.
26-5. Drink Delicious Coca-Cola, 1913.
26-6. Drink Coca-Cola, 1914.
26-7. A Distinctive Drink in a Distinctive Bottle, 1920.
26-8. A Pure Drink, 1930.
26-9. Fiftieth Anniversary, 1936.
26-10. Take Home a Carton, 1950.
26-11. World's Fair, New York, 1964.

26-2. Matchbook holder, 1906.

26-12. Match safe, 1908. Many people collect match safes of all types— embossed, engraved, or embroidered.

26-3. Matchbook holder, 1907.

26-13. Celluloid matchbook holder, 1910.

26-14. Silver ashtray, 1930.

26-17. Solid brass ashtray, fiftieth anniversary, 1936.

26-15. Cigarette box, frosted glass, fiftieth anniversary, 1936.

26-16. Four-suit ashtrays, 1940. Very popular and hard to find.

26-18. Crinkled ashtray, 1950.

26-19. Match holder ashtray, unique, 1940.

26-21. Can lighter, 1950.

26-20. Musical lighter, "Things go better with Coke," 1960.

26-22. Miniature lighter, 1950.

Thermometers

Many people collect thermometers exclusively. There are over one hundred different thermometers.

Other collectible thermometers not pictured include:

27-2. Wooden, 1900.
27-3. Wooden, 1905.
27-4. Tin bottle, 17", 1930.
27-5. Tin, oval with bottle, 7" × 16", 1936.
27-6. Tin bottle, 17", 1950.
27-7. Tin bottle, 17", 1958.

27-1. Two-bottled thermometer, 1941.

27-8. Drink Coca-Cola, 1939.

Toys

Toys not pictured:

28-1. Whistle, 1940.
28-2. Bank, 1948.
28-3. Cap bank, 1950.
28-4. Model plane, 1950.
28-5. Ping-Pong paddles, 1950.

28-8. Comic book, 1951.
28-9. Coke bank, 1960.
28-10. Magic kit, 1965.
28-11. Puzzle in a can, 1968.
28-12. Frisbee, 1970.
28-13. Beanbag, 1971.

28-6. American Flyer kit, 1930.

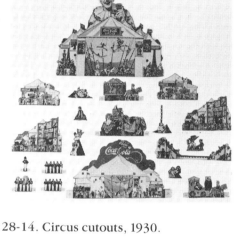

28-14. Circus cutouts, 1930.

28-7. Bingo, 1930.

28-15. Checkers, 1930.

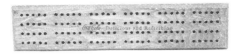

28-16. Cribbage board, 1930.

28-19. Dart board, 1935.

28-17. Toy stove, 1938.

28-18. Toy train car, 1938.

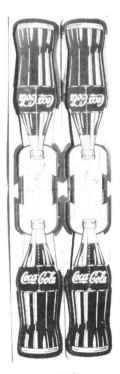

28-20. Boomerang, 1940.

28-21. Tick-tack-toe, 1940.

28-24. Marbles, 1950.

28-22. Darts, 1940.

28-25. Dominos, 1940.

28-23. Dispenser, 1960.

28-26. Yo-yo, 1960.

28-27. Bang gun, 1960.

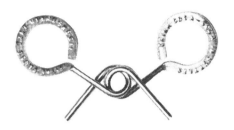

28-28. Puzzle, 1960.

28-29. Bingo, 1960.

Trays

Standard sizes for trays are: early, dated round, 9¹/₂″ diameter; matching round change trays, 5¹/₂″ diameter; and large ovals, 12¹/₂″ × 15¹/₄″. The rectangular trays were eventually standardized to measure 10¹/₂″ × 13¹/₄″. Trays illustrated are standard sizes unless otherwise noted.

29-1. Victorian girl, 1898.

29-2. Hilda Clark, 1899.
29-3. Matching change tray.

29-4. Hilda Clark, 9³/₄″ dia., 1900.
29-5. Matching change tray.

29-8. St. Louis Fair, 10³/₄″ dia., 1904.
29-9. Matching large oval,
13³/₄″ × 16¹/₂″.
29-10. Small change tray, 4″ × 6″.

29-6. Bottle tray, 9³/₄″ dia., 1900.
29-7. Matching change tray.

29-11. Hilda Clark, 9³/₄″ dia., 1903.
29-12. Matching change tray, 6″ dia.
29-13. Matching change tray 4″ dia.
29-14. Large 15″ × 18¹/₂″ tray.

29-15. Lillian Russell, 10¹/₂″ × 13″ oval, 1904. There is another version of this tray that shows a bottle displayed on the table in place of the glass.

29-19. Juanita, 10³/₄″ × 13¹/₄″ dia., 1905.

29-20. Matching change tray, 4″ dia.

29-16. Relieves Fatigue, 10¹/₂″ × 13″ oval, 1906.
29-17. Large oval.
29-18. Small change tray.

29-21. Coca-Cola girl, 1909.
29-22. Oval change tray.
29-23. Large oval.

29-26. Elaine, 8½" × 19", 1917.
29-27. Change tray. This tray shape was produced in 1917 only.

29-28. Betty, 1914.
29-29. Large oval.
29-30. Change tray.

29-26. Elaine, 8½" × 19", 1917.
29-27. Change tray.
This tray shape was produced in 1917 only.

29-31. Garden girl, 1920.
29-32. Large oval, 13¾" × 16½".
29-33. Change tray.

29-34. Summer girl, 1921.

29-36. Autumn girl, 1922.

29-35. Flapper girl, 1923.

29-37. Smiling girl, 1924.

29-38. Girl at party, 1925.

29-40. Sports couple, 1926.

29-39. Soda fountain clerk, 1927.

29-41. Curb service, 1927.

29-42. Girl with bobbed hair, 1927.

29-44. Girl in swimsuit holding glass, 1929.
29-45. Girl in swimsuit holding bottle (more unusual).

29-43. Girl with a telephone, 1930.

29-46. Bathing beauty, 1930.

29-47. Farm boy with dog, 1931.

29-49. Bathing beauty, 1932.

29-48. Francis Dee, 1933.

29-50. Maureen O'Sullivan and Johnny Weissmuller, 1934.

29-51. Madge Evans, 1935.

29-53. Hostess, 1936.

29-52. Running girl, 1937.

29-54. Girl in the afternoon, 1938.

29-57. Sailor girl, 1940.

29-55. Springboard girl, 1939.

29-56. Girl ice skater, 1941.

29-58. Two girls at car, 1941.

29-59. Girl with wind in her hair, 1943. .

29-61. Girl with menu, 1950. French version of this tray is worth more.

29-60. TV tray, 1956.

29-62. Girl with the umbrella, 1957.

29-63. Rooster tray, 1957.

29-65. Birdhouse tray, 1957.

29-64. Western Coca-Cola Bottling Company Vienna art plates, 1905. In 1905, the Vienna Art Company made a variety of plates advertising bakeries, taverns, haberdasheries, and Coca-Cola. The metal plates had very ornate frames and were packed in wooden, velvet-lined cases. Western Coca-Cola Bottling Company used the Vienna art plates for advertising instead of the conventional Coke trays. The company, in Chicago, Illinois, was a subsidiary of the Coca-Cola Company, and provided syrup and advertising items to bottlers within its territory. As Coke memorabilia, these trays are valuable simply because of the stamp on the back: "Vienna Art Plates, Pat. Feb. 21st 1905, Western Coca-Cola Bottling Co."

29-66. TV tray, picnic basket, 1958.

29-69. Pansy garden, 1961. Tray may be found with either "Coke refreshes you best" or "Be really refreshed."

29-67. Lillian Russell, 1968.
29-68. Lillian Russell, 1975, (not shown).

29-70. Lillian Nordica, 1969. Also a version in French.

29-71. 1909, reproduced in 1971.
Reproduction trays can be identified by
the date on the rim. Also, trademark
is not enclosed in the fishtail of the C
in the logo.

29-73. 1912, reproduced in 1972.

29-72. 1914, reproduced in 1972.

29-74. 1917, reproduced in 1972.

Wallets and coin purses

Collectible wallets not shown:

30-1. Wallet, 1912.

30-4. Embossed wallet, 1915.
30-5. Wallet, 1922.
30-6. Billfold, 1928.

30-2. Engraved coin purse, 1906.

30-7. Embossed coin purse, 1906.

30-3. Two-sided coin purse, 1910.

30-8. Change purse, 1910.

30-9. Billfold, 1912.

30-11. Wallet, 1919.

30-10. Wallet, 1970.

30-12. Embossed wallet, 1928.

Watch fobs

No one wore a wristwatch in the early 1900s. Instead, people wore pocket watches with watch fobs. The timepiece was attached to the fob with a piece of leather. The watch fobs were generally $1^3/_4'' \times 1^1/_4'' \times 1^1/_2''$.

Not pictured:
31-1. Girl sitting on bench, 1900.
31-4. Hilda Clark, 1900.
31-5. Oval, celluloid and metal, 1905.
31-6. Girl in car, $1^1/_2'' \times 2''$, 1906.
31-7. Girl with bottle, 1906.
31-8. Rectangle, metal Coca-Cola, 1908.
31-9. Drink Coca-Cola, 1925.

31-2. Silver or brass, 1908.

31-10. Metal, girl, 1917.

31-3. Metal, dogs, 1925.

Price Guide
(by Figure number)

No.	Price ($)
Blotters	
1-1	300
1-2	30
1-3	15
1-4	15
1-5	7
1-6	7
1-7	7
1-8	5
1-9	5
1-10	3
1-11	3
1-12	3
1-13	3
1-14	3
1-15	3
1-16	50
1-17	75
1-18	30
1-19	3
Bookmarks	
2-1	450
2-2	400
2-3	450
2-4	250
2-5	450
2-6	250
2-7	450
Books	
3-1	45
3-2	35
3-3	45
3-4	25
3-5	12
3-6	(ea.) 8
3-7	8
3-8	8
3-9	10
3-10	30
3-11	10
3-12	5
3-13	5
3-14	20
3-15	7
3-16	7
3-17	5

No.	Price ($)
Bottles	
4-1	150
4-2	100
4-3	150
4-4	250
4-5	225
4-6	300
4-7	275
4-8	275
4-9	175
4-10	125
4-11	100
4-12	10
4-13	60
Calendars	
5-1	6500
5-2	3600
5-3	3500
5-4	5000
5-5	2000
5-6	2500
5-7	2000
5-8	2000
5-9	3000
5-10	2500
5-11	1500
5-12	1000
5-13	1800
5-14	2500
5-15	2300
5-16	1500
5-17	700
5-18	1200
5-19	650
5-20	750
5-21	750
5-22	1000
5-23	750
5-24	750
5-25	500
5-26	550
5-27	350
5-28	400
5-29	400
5-30	475
5-31	475
5-32	375
5-33	550

No.	Price ($)
5-34	550
5-35	750
5-36	350
5-37	350
5-38	350
5-39	350
5-40	350
5-41	250
5-42	200
5-43	175
5-44	150
5-45	85
5-46	75
5-47	75
5-48	75
5-49	300
5-50	70
5-51	300
5-52	55
5-53	60
5-54	60
5-55	60
5-56	60
5-57	55
5-58	55
5-59	55
5-60	50
5-61	35
5-62	25
5-63	25
5-64	25
5-65	25
5-66	10
5-67	15
5-68	10
5-69	10
5-70	15
5-71	15
5-72	15
5-73	15
Cars and Trucks	
6-1	175
6-2	125
6-3	75
6-4	100
6-5	35
6-6	35
6-7	175
6-8	20

No.	Price ($)
6-9	50
6-10	15
6-11	1000
6-12	1200
6-13	175
6-14	50
6-15	45
6-16	75
6-17	125
6-18	125
6-19	325
6-20	50
6-21	50
6-22	40
6-23	100
6-24	25
6-25	30
6-26	25
6-27	25
6-28	40
6-29	25
6-30	20

Cartons and Bottle Holders

No.	Price ($)
7-1	175
7-2	25
7-3	75
7-4	35
7-5	25
7-6	20
7-7	30
7-8	25

Clocks

No.	Price ($)
8-1	5000
8-2	5000
8-3	450
8-4	500
8-5	2500
8-6	800
8-7	1000
8-8	700
8-9	650
8-10	40
8-11	40

Chewing Gum

No.	Price ($)
9-1	250
9-2	7500
9-3	35
9-4	50
9-5	250
9-6	600
9-7	200
9-8	4200
9-9	200

No.	Price ($)
9-10	750
9-11	750
9-12	50
9-13	650
9-14	450

Coolers and Miniatures

No.	Price ($)
10-1	45
10-2	50
10-3	750
10-4	750
10-5	350
10-6	45
10-7	10
10-8	5
10-9	25
10-10	35
10-11	35
10-12	10
10-13	35
10-14	35

Coupons

No.	Price ($)
11-1	400
11-2	400
11-3	300
11-4	350
11-5	175
11-6	175
11-7	175
11-8	75
11-9	40
11-10	10

Fans

No.	Price ($)
12-1	125
12-2	30
12-3	30

Glass Items and Lamps

No.	Price ($)
13-1	3000
13-2	1500
13-3	2500
13-4	3500
13-5	1500
13-6	700
13-7	700
13-8	150
13-9	5000
13-10	150
13-11	50
13-12	125
13-13	60

No.	Price ($)
13-14	150

Glasses

No.	Price ($)
14-1	325
14-2	325
14-3	350
14-4	35

Knives

No.	Price ($)
15-1	350
15-2	175
15-3	100
15-4	100
15-5	100

Miscellaneous

No.	Price ($)
16-1	300
16-2	35
16-3	15
16-4	175
16-5	275
16-6	75
16-7	65
16-8	75
16-9	15
16-10	250
16-11	15
16-12	35
16-13	10
16-14	30
16-15	30
16-16	600
16-17	150
16-18	100
16-19	100
16-20	100
16-21	125
16-22	75
16-23	40
16-24	200
16-25	25
16-26	250
16-27	15
16-28	125
16-29	400
16-30	200
16-31	150
16-32	35
16-33	45
16-34	10
16-35	35
16-36	35
16-37	200
16-38	100
16-39	300
16-40	75
16-41	150

No.	Price ($)	No.	Price ($)	No.	Price ($)
16-42	35	**Playing Cards**		**Records and Music**	
16-43	40				
16-44	30	19-1	850	23-1	500
16-45	25	19-2	600	23-2	750
16-46	35	19-3	250	23-3	150
16-47	10	19-4	50	23-4	25
16-48	150	19-5	40	23-5	25
16-49	35	19-6	30	23-6	5
16-50	125	19-7	30	23-7	15
16-51	20	19-8	50	23-8	4
16-52	30	19-9	25	23-9	7
16-53	10	19-10	20	23-10	(ea.) 25
16-54	35	19-11	20	23-11	40
16-55	35	19-12	15		
16-56	45	19-13	10	**Signs**	
16-57	55	19-14	15		
16-58	75	19-15	5	24-1	1500
16-59	75	19-16	4	24-2	1500
16-60	100	19-17	4	24-3	8000
16-61	175	19-18	4	24-4	1500
				24-5	4500
Openers		**Pocket Mirrors**		24-6	1800
				24-7	1600
17-1	250	20-1	375	24-8	1500
17-2	60	20-2	250	24-9	3000
17-3	50	20-3	300	24-10	3500
17-4	25	20-4	300	24-11	200
17-5	50	20-5	200	24-12	85
17-6	40	20-6	200	24-13	100
17-7	250	20-7	300	24-14	600
17-8	4	20-8	225	24-15	900
17-9	40	20-9	700	24-16	100
17-10	35	20-10	350	24-17	1200
17-11	40			24-18	50
17-12	5	**Postcards**		24-19	65
17-13	40			24-20	70
17-14	40	21-1	400	24-21	30
17-15	5	21-2	375	24-22	450
17-16	5	21-3	100	24-23	100
		21-4	100	24-24	100
Paper Items		21-5	100	24-25	125
		21-6	100	24-26	125
18-1	350	21-7	50	24-27	275
18-2	500	21-8	75	24-28	275
18-3	350	21-9	35	24-29	75
18-4	500	21-10	100	24-30	850
18-5	350	21-11	85	24-31	650
18-6	90	21-12	125	24-32	1500
18-7	125			24-33	750
18-8	40	**Radios**		24-34	350
18-9	75			24-35	125
18-10	50	22-1	1450	24-36	400
18-11	40	22-2	450	24-37	75
18-12	10	22-3	175	24-38	100
18-13	7	22-4	85	24-39	100
18-14	50	22-5	85	24-40	250
18-15	75	22-6	15	24-41	50
18-16	5	22-7	65	24-42	40
				24-43	75

No.	Price ($)	No.	Price ($)	No.	Price ($)
24-44	100	28-3	10	29-31	450
24-45	75	28-4	25	29-32	500
24-46	150	28-5	30	29-33	250
		28-6	250	29-34	450
		28-7	25	29-35	250

Festoons

No.	Price ($)
25-1	400
25-2	150
25-3	100
25-4	100
25-5	100
25-6	100
25-7	100
25-8	350
25-9	400
25-10	400
25-11	300

Smoking Paraphernalia

No.	Price ($)
26-1	200
26-2	125
26-3	125
26-4	175
26-5	250
26-6	250
26-7	50
26-8	10
26-9	10
26-10	2
26-11	2
26-12	300
26-13	100
26-14	15
26-15	275
26-16	150
26-17	25
26-18	20
26-19	325
26-20	35
26-21	30
26-22	20

Thermometers

No.	Price ($)
27-1	100
27-2	275
27-3	275
27-4	100
27-5	85
27-6	40
27-7	25
27-8	85

Toys

No.	Price ($)
28-1	35
28-2	15

No.	Price ($)
28-8	35
28-9	7
28-10	35
28-11	25
28-12	10
28-13	20
28-14	50
28-15	35
28-16	45
28-17	500
28-18	150
28-19	45
28-20	10
28-21	65
28-22	30
28-23	75
28-24	30
28-25	40
28-26	25
28-27	20
28-28	20
28-29	5

Trays

No.	Price ($)
29-1	6500
29-2	5000
29-3	2500
29-4	3500
29-5	2000
29-6	5000
29-7	2500
29-8	1200
29-9	1400
29-10	275
29-11	3000
29-12	750
29-13	600
29-14	2500
29-15	1700
29-16	1200
29-17	850
29-18	350
29-19	350
29-20	350
29-21	500
29-22	275
29-23	850
29-24	400
29-25	250
29-26	200
29-27	175
29-28	350
29-29	250
29-30	200

No.	Price ($)
29-36	450
29-37	375
29-38	250
29-39	275
29-40	350
29-41	300
29-42	300
29-43	175
29-44	250
29-45	300
29-46	175
29-47	400
29-48	275
29-49	300
29-50	475
29-51	200
29-52	100
29-53	185
29-54	85
29-55	125
29-56	125
29-57	125
29-58	85
29-59	40
29-60	25
29-61	40
29-62	150
29-63	75
29-64	(ea.) 350–500
29-65	75
29-66	35
29-67	50
29-68	10
29-69	25
29-70	35
29-71	10
29-72	10
29-73	10
29-74	10

Wallets and Coin Purses

No.	Price ($)
30-1	90
30-2	75
30-3	125
30-4	60
30-5	75
30-6	50
30-7	100
30-8	75
30-9	75
30-10	20
30-11	75
30-12	25

Watch Fobs

No.	Price ($)
31-1	450
31-2	100
31-3	100
31-4	450
31-5	450
31-6	400
31-7	400
31-8	150
31-9	125
31-10	400

Items in Color Section

No.	Price ($)
1	4500
2	4000
3	7000
4	3000
5	500
6	275
7	250
8	100
9	275
10	400
11	500
12	100
13	1500

Source directory

Books

Coca-Cola, An Illustrated History, Pat Watters, 1978, Doubleday and Company, Garden City, NY.

Excellent look into the strategy behind the building of the Coke empire.

Coca-Cola Collectibles, Volumes I-IV, Shelly and Helen Goldstein, 1970, 1973, 1974, 1975, P.O. Box 381, Independence, OR 97351.

Features hundreds of full-color photographs. These books are widely used and referred to in correspondence, trading, and advertising by collectors around the world.

Golson's Unique and Varied Bottles, Golson Hook, 75 Roswell Street, Alpharetta, GA 30201.

Lists the values of bottles from most local bottlers.

The Illustrated Guide to the Collectibles of Coca-Cola, Cecil Munsey, 1972, Hawthorn Books, NY.

A good accounting of Coca-Cola history. Some photographs.

The Index of Coca-Cola Collectibles, Shelly and Helen Goldstein, 1982, P.O. Box 381, Independence, OR 97351.

An updated price guide and index, this book is designed to be used alone or with the four *Coca-Cola Collectibles* volumes. Each item is indexed alphabetically and cross-referenced by date. Includes fifty full-color photographs.

Monthly Publications

American Collector
Drawer C
Kermit, TX 79745

Provides a broad market in which one can advertise collectibles.

The Antique Trader
P.O. Box 1050
Dubuque, IA 52001

An excellent newspaper for collectors of everything.

Rarities
P.O. Box 667
Beaumont, CA 92223

A general hobby magazine.

Other publications are available from these two companies:

The Nostalgia Company
21 South Lake Drive
Hackensack, NJ 07601

This company sponsors a mail-order auction. For four dollars you receive three auction catalogs that describe Coca-Cola, Pepsi Cola, Hires, Orange Crush, and Moxie advertising collectibles.

Palmetto Warehouse
Highway 321
Norway, SC 29113

Write for catalog of novelty Coke items.

Note: There are some mail order auction houses that do not grade the condition of sale items. Always try to establish an accurate description of items you intend to buy through the mail.

Museums

Calamity Jane's Ice Cream House
  and Coca-Cola Museum
Sam's Town
5111 Boulder Highway
Las Vegas, NV
(800) 634-6371

This ice cream house and museum is one of a kind. The nostalgic soda fountain is decorated with the most elite collectibles, including three glass chandeliers, a solid brass cash register, and several porcelain syrup dispensers. More than three hundred items are permanently displayed for view from 10 a.m. to 1 a.m. They also serve marvelous ice cream made from the finest ingredients.

Schmidt's Marvelous Museum
Elizabethtown, KY
(502) 737-4000

The Schmidt Museum is located in the Coca-Cola Bottling Company in Elizabethtown. After touring the museum, visitors have a chance to view modern bottling procedures. The Museum is open Monday through Friday from 9 a.m. to 4 p.m.

Antiques Stores

Antique Gas Pumps
896 South West 62 Avenue
North Lauderdale, FL 33068

Antique Supermarket
84 Wooster Street
New York, NY 10012

Charro & Company
10700 Hammerly, Suite 102
Houston, TX 77043
(713) 464-6911
   Open six days a week, sells
advertising antiques of all kinds.

Classic Collectibles
198 North Parkway
Jackson, TN 38305
(901) 668-5522
   Open 10–6 Mon–Sat.

Country Corner Flea Market
585 North Jefferson
Lebanon, MO 65536
(417) 588-1430
   Open seven days a week.

County Line Antiques
Box 1439
Aldergrove, BC V0X1A0

Covered Wagon Trading Post
Route 3, Box 156
Daleville, AL 36322

Curtis & MacKnight Antiques
426 North 19th Street
Houston, TX 77008
(713) 862-8638
   Open four to five days a week,
sells advertising antiques.

Hob Knob Shop
Knob Lick, MO 63651

Jennings Collectibles
2120 Metro Circle
Huntsville, AL 35801

Mar Van Antiques
2803 North Big Spring Street
Midland, TX 79705

MariMac Antiques
103 South Church Lane
Tappahannock, VA 22560

McMurray Antiques
Box 404
Windsor, NY 13865

National Pop Can Collectors Club
NPCCC
P.O. Box 7862
Rockford, IL 61126
(815) 874-5915

Pearl Brown Antiques
535 Whalley Avenue
New Haven, CT 06511

Royal Peddler
1020 Auahi Street
Honolulu, HI 96814

Southeastern Antiques
141 North Myrtle
Jacksonville, FL 32204

Soda Mart
Ridgecrest Drive
Goodlettsville, TN 37072
(615) 859-5236

The Coca-Cola Collectors Club

The Coca-Cola Collectors Club International (formerly The Cola Clan) is a non-profit organization for collectors and their families who are interested in the history and the memorabilia of The Coca-Cola Company.

The Coca-Cola Collectors Club International provides:

- International communication among nearly 6000 collectors
- Markets for buying, trading and selling collectibles
- Informative monthly newsletter with free classified ads for members
- Special monthly merchandise offerings for members
- Regional chapters
- Annual international and regional conventions
- Yearly membership directory

The Coca-Cola Collectors Club is not sponsored by The Coca-Cola Company, and is run by volunteers elected annually from the membership by mail ballot (all primary and associate members may run for elective office). For information on annual dues for membership, write to:

The Coca-Cola Collectors Club International
P.O. Box 49166
Atlanta, Georgia 30359-1166

Coca-Cola bottling companies

Coca-Cola bottling companies are responsible for bringing the refreshment and enjoyment of Coca-Cola to people in their local communities. A list of these bottling companies arranged by state follows. Within each state, bottling companies are listed in alphabetical order according to the cities in which they are located. This list is from the 1990–1991 National Soft Drink Association's directory of active members.

ALABAMA

Birmingham

Birmingham Coca-Cola Bottling Co.
4600 East Lake Boulevard 35217
Mailing address; P.O. Box 2006
   Birmingham, AL 35201
205/841-2653

Decatur

Decatur Coca-Cola Bottling Company
#1 Refreshment Place 35602
Mailing address: P.O. Box 1687
   Decatur, AL 35602
205/353-9211

Coca-Cola's Central Avenue headquarters in Los Angeles, with its famed Flagship facade, has long been a Los Angeles landmark. While the interior of the building was almost completely remodeled during 1975 and 1976 to create pleasant surroundings and accommodate future expansion, a particular point was made of preserving the best of the old in architectural details and design. This facade has now been dedicated as a historic monument—a symbol of the city's cultural and economic heritage.

Dothan

Coca-Cola Bottling Company
308 North St. Andrews Street
   36302
Mailing address: P.O. Box 1009
   Dothan, AL 36302

Florence

Coca-Cola Bottling Company
   Southeast Inc.
502-14 South Court Street 35631
Mailing address: P.O. Box 895
   Florence, AL 35631
205/764-5921

Huntsville

Huntsville Coca-Cola Bottling
   Company
514 Clinton Avenue, West 35802
Mailing address: P.O. Box 2709
   Huntsville, AL 35804-2709
205/533-9450

Montgomery

Coca-Cola Bottling Company
300 Coca-Cola Road 36105
Mailing address: P.O. Box 1830
   Montgomery, AL 36197-2301
205/284-9555

151

Oxford

Alabama Coca-Cola Bottling
  Company
701 West Hamric Drive
Highway 78 West 36203
Mailing address: P.O. Box 3539
  Oxford, AL 36203

Selma

Selma Coca-Cola Bottling Company
112 Green Street 36702
Mailing address: P.O. Box 1100
  Selma, AL 36702

Tillman's Corner

Coca-Cola Bottling Company of
  Mobile, Inc.
5300 Coca-Cola Road 36619
Mailing address: P.O. Box 190129
  Mobile, AL 36619-0129
205/666-2410

Troy

Montgomery Coca-Cola Bottling
  Co.
South Brundidge Street 36081
Mailing address: P.O. Box 142
  Troy, AL 36081

Tuscaloosa

Coca-Cola Bottling Company
2301 Eighth Street 35403
Mailing address: P.O. Box 1158
  Tuscaloosa, AL 35403

ALASKA

Ketchikan

Ketchikan Soda Works
3340 Tongass Avenue 99901
Mailing address: P.O. Box 7600
  Ketchikan, AK 99901
907/225-2470

Sitka

Sitka Bottling Company
1100 Halibut Point Road 99836
Mailing address: P.O. Box 197
  Sitka, AK 99836
907/747-3417

ARIZONA

Flagstaff

Northern Arizona Coca-Cola
  Bottling Company
3825 East Huntington 86002
Mailing address: P.O. Box 413
  Flagstaff, AZ 86002

Showlow

Northern Arizona Coca-Cola
  Bottling Company
P.O. Box 818 85901

Tempe

Phoenix Coca-Cola Bottling
  Company
1850 West Elliott Road 85284
Mailing address: P.O. Box 20008
  Phoenix, AZ 85036
602/831-0400

Tucson

Coca-Cola Bottling Company of
  Tucson, Inc.
3939 North Romero Road 85705
Mailing address: P.O. Box 1192
  San Angelo, TX 76902
602/887-1600

Winslow

Northern Arizona Coca-Cola
  Bottling Company
1941 West Second Street 86047
Mailing address: P.O. Box 38
  Winslow, AZ 86047

Yuma

Southwestern Ice & Coca-Cola
  Bottling Company
429-39 Gila Street 85364
Mailing address: P.O. Box 1988
  Yuma, AZ 85364

ARKANSAS

Batesville

Coca-Cola Bottling Company of
  Arkansas
100 East College Street 72501
Mailing address: P.O. Box 2014
  Batesville, AR 72501

Fort Smith

The Coca-Cola Bottling Company
  of Fort Smith
3600 Phoenix Avenue 72906
Mailing address: P.O. Box 6607
  Fort Smith, AR 72906
501/646-0571

Hot Springs

Coca-Cola Bottling Company of
  Hot Springs, Inc.
321 Market Street 71901
501/623-7707

Jonesboro

Coca-Cola Bottling Company of
  Northeast Arkansas, Inc.
2215 East Highland Drive 72401
Mailing address: P.O. Box 1660
  Jonesboro, AR 72403
501/932-6601

Little Rock

Coca-Cola Bottling Company of
  Arkansas
7000 Interstate 30 72209
Mailing address: P.O. Box 3508
  Little Rock, AR 72203
501/569-2700

Magnolia

Magnolia Coca-Cola Bottling
  Company, Inc.
114 South Madison Street 71753
Mailing address: P.O. Box 278
  Magnolia, AR 71753
501/234-1272

Monticello

Coca-Cola Bottling Company of
  South Arkansas
Highways 81 & 4 71655
Mailing address: P.O. Box 466
  Monticello, AR 71655

Nashville

Coca-Cola Bottling Company of
  Nashville, Arkansas
Highway 27 South 71852
Mailing address: P.O. Box 1560
  Nashville, AR 71852
501/845-2262

Pine Bluff

Coca-Cola Bottling Company of
  South Arkansas
205 East Second Street 71611
Mailing address: P.O. Box 6668
  Pine Bluff, AR 71611

Searcy

Coca-Cola Bottling Company of
  Arkansas
510 E. Lincoln Avenue 72143
Mailing address: P.O. Box 139
  Searcy, AR 72143

West Memphis

Canners of Eastern Arkansas, Inc.
1400 Rainier Road 72301
Mailing address: P.O. Box 1030
  West Memphis, AR 72303
501/732-1460

CALIFORNIA

Bakersfield

Coca-Cola Bottling Company of
  Los Angeles, Bakersfield Branch
414 19th Street 93301
Mailing address: 1334 South
  Central Avenue
  Los Angeles, CA 90021

Barstow

Coca-Cola Bottling Company
26777 West Main Street 92311

Blythe

Coca-Cola Bottling Company
190 South Main Street 92225
Mailing address: P.O. Box
  Drawer N
  Blythe, CA 92225

Downey

Coca-Cola Bottling Company of
  Los Angeles
8729 Cleta Street 90241
213/923-7202

Eureka

Coca-Cola Bottling Co. of Oregon
  Northern California Div., Eureka
1335 Albee Street 95501

Los Angeles

Coca-Cola Enterprises-West
1334 South Central Avenue 90021
213/746-5555

Marysville

Coca-Cola Bottling Co. of Oregon
  No. California Div., Marysville
1340 Melody Road 95901

Modesto

Modesto Coca-Cola Bottling
  Company
1520 Princeton Avenue 95350

Oakland

The Coca-Cola Bottling Company
  of California
1340 Cypress Street 94604

Sacramento

Sacramento Coca-Cola Bottling
  Company
2200 Stockton Boulevard 95817
Mailing address: P.O. Box 160608
  Sacramento, CA 95819
916/456-6464

Salinas

Coca-Cola Bottling Company of
  California
251 West Market Street 93901
Mailing address: P.O. Box 2119
  Salinas, CA 93902

San Diego

Coca-Cola Bottling Company of
  San Diego
1348 47th Street 92102
Mailing address: P.O. Box X-8000
  San Diego, CA 92102
619/262-7551

San Francisco

Coca-Cola Bottling Company of
  California
1560 Mission Street 94103
Mailing address: P.O. Box 888
  San Francisco, CA 94101

San Jose

Coca-Cola Bottling Company of
  California
1555 Old Bayshore Highway 95112
Mailing address: P.O. Box 1840
  San Jose, CA 95109

San Leandro

Coca-Cola Bottling Company of
  California
14655 Wicks Boulevard 94577
415/667-6300

Santa Cruz

Coca-Cola Bottling Company of
  California
6100 Soquel Avenue 95060
Mailing address: P.O. Box 1840
  San Jose, CA 95109

Stockton

Coca-Cola Bottling Company
1100 North Wilson Drive 95205

Ukiah

Ukiah Coca-Cola Bottling Company
650 Babcock Lane 95482

Ventura

Coca-Cola Bottling Company of
  Los Angeles (Ventura Branch)
5335 Walker Street 93003
Mailing address: 1334 South
  Central Avenue
  Los Angeles, CA 90021

COLORADO

Colorado Springs

Wichita Coca-Cola Bottling
  Company
415-17 West Pikes Peak Avenue
80905
719/633-2653

Denver

Denver Coca-Cola Bottling
  Company
3800 Race Street 80205
Mailing address: P.O. Box 17100
  Denver, CO 80217
303/292-2653

Durango

Durango Coca-Cola Bottling
  Company
7th & Camino del Rio 81301
Mailing address: P.O. Box 760
  Durango, CO 81302
303/247-1560

155

Grand Junction

Coca-Cola Bottling Company of
  Grand Junction
1226 Winters Avenue 81502

Greeley

Denver Coca-Cola Bottling
  Company, Greeley Center
1200 Seventh Avenue 80631

Pueblo

Pueblo Coca-Cola Bottling
  Company
3004 South Prairie 81005

Salida

The Salida Coca-Cola Bottling Co.
1320 D Street 81201
Mailing address: P.O. Box 1034
  Salida, CO 81201

CONNECTICUT

East Hartford

The Coca-Cola Bottling Company
  of New York
451 Main Street 06108
203/569-7730

Fairfield

The Coca-Cola Bottling Company
  of New York
450 Scofield Avenue 06430

Middletown

Coca-Cola Bottling Company of
  Middletown
310 South Main Street 06457

New London

Coca-Cola Bottling Company of
  Southeastern New England, Inc.
951 Bank Street 06320
Mailing address: P.O. Box 1310
  New London, CT 06320
203/443-2816

DELAWARE

Dover

Dover Coca-Cola Bottling
  Company
Lincoln Street 19903
Mailing address: P.O. Box 306
  Dover, DE 19903
302/734-2651

FLORIDA

Cocoa

Brevard Coca-Cola Bottling
  Company
695 Clearlake Road 32922

Daytona Beach

Florida Coca-Cola Bottling
  Company
327 Orange Avenue 32115
Mailing address: P.O. Box 2249
  Daytona Beach, FL 32115
904/258-3355

Fort Myers

Fort Myers Coca-Cola Bottling
  Company
2403 Cleveland Avenue 33902
Mailing address: P.O. Box 700
  Fort Myers, FL 33902
813/332-1242

Ft. Pierce

Ft. Pierce Coca-Cola Bottling
Company
3939 St. Lucie Boulevard 34946
Mailing address: P.O. Box 428
Ft. Pierce, FL 34946

Gainesville

Gainesville Coca-Cola Bottling
Company
929 East University Avenue 32601

Hollywood

The Coca-Cola Bottling Company
of Miami, Inc.
3350 Pembroke Road 33021
305/985-5081

Homestead

Homestead Coca-Cola Bottling
Company
186 Southwest First Street 33030

Jacksonville

Jacksonville Coca-Cola Bottling
Company
1411 Huron Street 32205
Mailing address: P.O. Box 37619
Jacksonville, FL 32205
904/786-2720

Lake City

Lake City Coca-Cola Bottling Co.
900 N. Alachua Street 32055
Mailing address: P.O. Box 1568
Lake City, FL 32055

Lakeland

Lakeland Coca-Cola Bottling
Company, Inc.
S-540 at Reynolds Road 33802
Mailing address: P.O. Drawer AE
Lakeland, FL 33802

Leesburg

Leesburg Coca-Cola Bottling
Company
110 S. Highway 468 34748
Mailing address: P.O. Box 1219
Leesburg, FL 34748

Marianna

Marianna Coca-Cola Bottling
Company
Highway 90 West 32446
Mailing address: P.O. Box 918
Marianna, FL 32446

Miami

The Coca-Cola Bottling Company
of Miami, Inc.
301 Northwest 29th Street 33127

Ocala

Ocala Coca-Cola Bottling Company
2870 N.E. 24th Street 32670

Orlando

Florida Coca-Cola Bottling
Company
2900 Mercy Drive 32805
305/295-9290

Panama City

Panama City Coca-Cola Bottling
Company
238 West Fifth Street 32401
Mailing address: P.O. Box 846
Panama City, FL 32401

Pensacola

Hygeia Coca-Cola Bottling
  Company
7330 North Davis Highway 32504
Mailing address: P.O. Drawer
  12630
  Pensacola, FL 32574
904/478-4800

Perry

Perry Coca-Cola Bottling Company
Highway 98 32347
Mailing address: P.O. Box 839
  Perry, FL 32347

Punta Gorda

Punta Gorda Coca-Cola Bottling
  Co.
3015 Cooper Street 33950
Mailing address: P.O. Box 937
  Punta Gorda, FL 33950

Quincy

Quincy Coca-Cola Bottling
  Company
305 West Crawford Street 32351
Mailing address: P.O. Box 270
  Quincy, FL 32351

Sarasota

Sarasota Coca-Cola Bottling
  Company
1126 North Lime Avenue 34237
Mailing address: P.O. Box 3948
  Sarasota, FL 34237

St. Augustine

St. Augustine Coca-Cola Bottling
  Company
1 Coke Drive & State Road 312
  32086

St. Petersburg

St. Petersburg Coca-Cola Bottling
  Company
2950 Grandy Bridge Boulevard
  33742
Mailing address: P.O. Box 20043
  St. Petersburg, FL 33702

Tallahassee

Florida Coca-Cola Bottling
  Company
1320 South Monroe Street
Northwest Unit 32301

Tampa

Tampa Coca-Cola Bottling
  Company
9102 Sabal Industrial Blvd. 33169
813/623-5411

Tarpon Springs

Tarpon Springs Coca-Cola Bottling
  Company
4875 US Alt. Hwy. 19 S. 34689
Mailing address: P.O. Box 536
  Tarpon Springs, FL 34689
813/937-5181

Valparaiso

Hygeia Coca-Cola Bottling
  Company
647 State Highway 85 32580

GEORGIA

Albany

Albany Coca-Cola Bottling
  Company
925 Pine Avenue 31701
Mailing address: P.O. Box 47
  Albany, GA 31701

Athens

The Athens Coca-Cola Bottling
  Company
297 Prince Avenue 30603
Mailing address: P.O. Box 872
  Athens, GA 30603

Atlanta

The Atlanta Coca-Cola Bottling
  Company
100 Galleria Parkway, N.W.
Suite 800 30339
Mailing address: P.O. Box 4268
  Atlanta, GA 30302
404/852-7000

Augusta

Augusta Coca-Cola Bottling
  Company
1901 North Leg Road 30914
Mailing address: P.O. Box 15029
  Augusta, GA 30919-5029
404/736-2211

Brunswick

Coca-Cola Bottling Company
  Brunswick Sales Center
508 Mansfield Street 31520
Mailing address: P.O. Drawer C
  Brunswick, GA 31520

Carrollton

Carrollton Coca-Cola Bottling
  Company
217 Alabama Street 30117
Mailing address: P.O. Box 249
  Carrollton, GA 30117

Claxton

Coca-Cola Bottling Company
  Claxton Sales Center
614 West Main Street 30417
Mailing address: P.O. Box 338
  Claxton, GA 30417

College Park

The Atlanta Coca-Cola Bottling
  Company
4755 Edison Drive 30337

Columbus

Columbus Coca-Cola Bottling
  Company
6055 Coca-Cola Boulevard 31909
Mailing address: P.O. Box 7667
  Columbus, GA 31909-7667

Cornelia

Cornelia Coca-Cola Bottling
  Company
501 North Main Street 30531

Dalton

Dalton Coca-Cola Bottling
  Company
1000 South Thornton Avenue
  30720
Mailing address: P.O. Box 671
  Dalton, GA 30722

Decatur

The Atlanta Coca-Cola Bottling
  Company
2400 Mellon Court 300

Dublin

The Atlanta Coca-Cola Bottling
  Company
415 East Jackson Street 31021
Mailing address: P.O. Box 674
  Dublin, GA 31021

Gainesville

The Atlanta Coca-Cola Bottling
  Company
C-15 Brown Bridge Road 30503
Mailing address: P.O. Box 656
  Gainesville, GA 30501

Griffin

The Atlanta Coca-Cola Bottling
  Company
410 East Taylor Street 30223

Jasper

The Atlanta Coca-Cola Bottling
  Company
670 Church Street 30143
Mailing address: P.O. Box 117
  Jasper, GA 30143

Lawrenceville

The Atlanta Coca-Cola Bottling
  Company
924 Buford Drive 30243

Macon

The Atlanta Coca-Cola Bottling
  Company
440 Oak Street 31208
Mailing address: P.O. Box 4144
  Macon, GA 31213

Manchester

Coca-Cola Bottling Company
  Manchester Sales Center
111 North 5th Avenue 31816

Marietta

The Atlanta Coca-Cola Bottling
  Company
1091 Industrial Park Dr., N.E.
  30062
404/424-9080

Savannah

Coca-Cola Bottling Company
  Savannah Sales Center
102 Coleman Boulevard 31408
Mailing address: P.O. Drawer 1110
  Pooler, GA 31322

Thomasville

Thomasville Coca-Cola Bottling
  Company
1017 East Jackson Street 31792
Mailing address: P.O. Box 737
  Thomasville, GA 31799
912/226-2136

Valdosta

Valdosta Coca-Cola Bottling Works
1408 North Ashley Street 31603
Mailing address: P.O. Box 189
  Valdosta, GA 31603

Warner Robins

The Atlanta Coca-Cola Bottling
  Company
98 Green Street 31093

Waycross

Coca-Cola Bottling Company
  Waycross-Douglas Sales Center
101 North Nichols Street 31501
Mailing address: P.O. Box 44
  Waycross, GA 31501

West Point

Coca-Cola Bottling Company of
  West Point-LaGrange
1700 East Tenth Street 31833
Mailing address: P.O. Box 530
  West Point, GA 31833-0530

HAWAII

Honolulu

Coca-Cola Bottling Company of
  Hawaii
949 Mapunapuna Street 96820
Mailing address: P.O. Box 30068
  Honolulu, HI 96820
808/839-6711

IDAHO

Idaho Falls

Coca-Cola Bottling Company of
  Idaho Falls
900 East Lincoln Road 83401
Mailing address: P.O. Box 2269
  Idaho Falls, ID 83403-2269

Lewiston

Coca-Cola Bottling Company
3010 Main 83501
Mailing address: P.O. Box 607
  Lewiston, ID 83501
208/746-0541

Pocatello

Coca-Cola Bottling Company of
  Pocatello
1003 North Main Street 83204

Twin Falls

Twin Falls Coca-Cola Bottling
  Company
248 Third Street, South 83301
Mailing address: P.O. Box 86
  Twin Falls, ID 83303

ILLINOIS

Alsip

Coca-Cola Bottling Co. of Chicago
  Alsip Manufacturing Division
12200 South Laramie Avenue
  60658
312/597-4700

Chicago

Coca-Cola Btlg Co.-Chicago-
  Wisconsin-Indianapolis-
  Keystone-Rochester
7400 North Oak Park Avenue
  60648
312/775-0900

Peru

Peru Coca-Cola Bottling Company
2325 Fourth Street 61354

Rockford

Coca-Cola Bottling Company of
  Mid-America
10400 North Second Street 61111

Springfield

Central States Coca-Cola Bottling
  Company
3495 Sangamon Avenue 62707
217/544-4891

St. Charles

Coca-Cola Bottling Company of
  Chicago
St. Charles Sales Center
Route 64 & Dunham Road 60174

Streator

Streator Coca-Cola Bottling
  Company
1109 North Bloomington Street
  61364
815/672-2434

INDIANA

Anderson

Coca-Cola Bottling Company of
  Indiana
Anderson Sales Center
3200 East 38th Street 46013

Columbus

Coca-Cola Bottling Company, Inc.
1334 Washington Street 47201
Mailing address: P.O. Box 567
  Columbus, IN 47202
812/376-3381

Evansville

Coca-Cola Bottling Company of
  Evansville
927 Pennsylvania Street 47730

Jasper

Coca-Cola Bottling Company of
  Jasper
Highway #231 South 47547
Mailing address: P.O. Box 109
  Jasper, IN 47547

Kokomo

Coca-Cola Bottling Company of
  Kokomo Indiana, Inc.
2305 North Davis Road 46901
Mailing address: P.O. Box 1049
  Kokomo, IN 46903
317/457-4421

Lafayette

Coca-Cola Bottling Company of
  Indiana
Lafayette Sales Center
830 North Sixth Street 47904
Mailing address: P.O. Box 1458
  Lafayette, IN 47904

Portland

Coca-Cola Bottling Company of
  Indiana
Portland Sales Center
1617 North Meridian Street 47371
219/726-7126

Richmond

Coca-Cola Bottling Company of
  Indiana
Richmond Sales Center
110 West Main Street 47374

Shelbyville

Coca-Cola Bottling Company of
  Indiana
Shelbyville Sales Center
405 North Harrison Street 46176

South Bend

Coca-Cola Bottling Company of
  Indiana
South Bend Sales Center
1818 Mishawaka Avenue 46615

Speedway

Coca-Cola Bottling Company of
   Indiana
   Indianapolis Mfg. & Sales Center
5000 West 25th Street 46224
317/243-3771

Tell City

Tell City Coca-Cola Bottling
   Company, Inc.
321 Ninth Street 47586
Mailing address: P.O. Box 425
   Tell City, IN 47586
812/547-6477

Terre Haute

Coca-Cola Bottling Company of
   Indiana
   Terre Haute Sales Center
924 Lafayette Avenue 47804

IOWA

Atlantic

Atlantic Bottling Company
4 East Second Street 50022
Mailing address: P.O. Box 110
   Atlantic, IA 50022
712/243-1440

Cedar Rapids

Coca-Cola Bottling Company of
   Cedar Rapids
851 66th Street 52404

Davenport

Coca-Cola Bottling Company of
   Mid-America
3750 West River Drive 52802

Mason City

Coca-Cola Bottling Company
2000 15th Street, Southwest 50401

Sioux City

Chesterman Company
4700 South Lewis Boulevard 51102
Mailing address: P.O. Box 3657
   Sioux City, IA 51102
712/255-8814

Waterloo

Coca-Cola Bottling Company of
   Mid-America
120 Washington Street 50701

KANSAS

Fort Scott

Fort Scott Coca-Cola Bottling Co.
2522 Richard Road 66701

Garden City

Garden City Coca-Cola Bottling
   Company
P.O. Box 816 67846

Lenexa

Coca-Cola Bottling Company of
   Mid-America, Inc.
9000 Marshall Drive 66215
Mailing address: P.O. Box 500
   Lenexa, KS 66201
913/492-8100

Mid America Container
   Corporation
10001 Industrial Boulevard 66215
913/888-3505

Salina

Salina Coca-Cola Bottling Company
240 Berg Road 67401

Wichita

Wichita Coca-Cola Bottling
  Company
3001 East Harry Street 67211
Mailing address: P.O. Box 365
  Wichita, KS 67201
316/682-1553

Winfield

The Coca-Cola Bottling Company
  of Winfield
1215 Main Street 67156
316/221-2710

KENTUCKY

Campbellsville

Coca-Cola Bottling Company of
  Campbellsville, Inc.
Highway 3183 42718
Mailing address: P.O. Box 10
  Campbellsville, KY 42719
502/465-4157

Lexington

Bluegrass Coca-Cola Bottling Co.
Leestown Road & Greendale Rd
  40582
Mailing address: P.O. Box 12330
  Lexington, KY 40582

Louisville

Bluegrass Coca-Cola Bottling
  Company
1661 West Hill Street 40210
Mailing address: P.O. Box 169002
  Louisville, KY 40216-9002
502/776-4651

Middlesboro

Middlesboro Coca-Cola Bottling,
  Inc.
1324 Cumberland Avenue 40965
Mailing address: P.O. Box 1485
  Middlesboro, KY 40965
606/248-2660

Paducah

Mid-States Coca-Cola Bottling
  Group
3141 Broadway 42001
Mailing address: P.O. Box 7909
  Paducah, KY 42001

Shelbyville

Coca-Cola Bottling Company
Highway 53, 1 Mile North I-64
  40066
Mailing address: P.O. Box 519
  Shelbyville, KY 40066
502/633-2653

LOUISIANA

Alexandria

Alexandria Coca-Cola Bottling
  Company, Ltd.
7400 Coliseum Boulevard 71303
Mailing address: P.O. Box 7027
  Alexandria, LA 71306
318/445-5555

Baton Rouge

Gulf Coast Coca-Cola Bottling
  Company, Inc.
10000 Dawnadele Avenue 70809-
  2586
504/293-2570

Bunkie

Bunkie Coca-Cola Bottling
   Company, Inc.
608 Southwest Main Street 71322
Mailing address: P.O. Box 599
   Bunkie, LA 71322
318/346-6614

Gretna

The Louisiana Coca-Cola Bottling
   Company
1000 Burmaster 70053

Lafayette

Coca-Cola Bottling Company
   Lafayette Sales Center
1314 Eraste Landry Road 70501
Mailing address: P.O. Box 3521
   Lafayette, LA 70502

Leesville

Coca-Cola Bottling Company of
   Leesville
201 East Murphy Street 71446
Mailing address: P.O. Box 590
   Leesville, LA 71446

Minden

Coca-Cola Bottling Company of
   Minden, Inc.
412 Pine Street 71055
Mailing address: P.O. Box 893
   Minden, LA 71058
318/377-6846

Natchitoches

Coca-Cola Bottling Company of
   Natchitoches
300 Parkway Drive 71457
Mailing address: P.O. Box 2118
   Natchitoches, LA 71457

New Iberia

Evangeline Coca-Cola Bottling
   Company, Inc.
401 West Admiral Doyle Drive
   70560
Mailing address: P.O. Drawer 9650
   New Iberia, LA 70562-9650

New Orleans

The Louisiana Coca-Cola Bottling
   Company, Ltd.
1050 S. Jefferson Davis Pkwy.
   70150
Mailing address: P.O. Box 50400
   New Orleans, LA 70150
504/822-2400

Ruston

Ruston Coca-Cola Bottling
   Company, Inc.
103 South Bonner Street 71270
Mailing address: P.O. Drawer 809
   Ruston, LA 71273
318/255-3997

Shreveport

Coca-Cola Bottling Company of
   Shreveport
305 Stoner Avenue 71101
Mailing address: P.O. Box 1114
   Shreveport, LA 71163
318/429-0205

Thibodaux

The Louisiana Coca-Cola Bottling
   Company, Ltd.
1300 Lynn Avenue 70301-0349
Mailing address: P.O. Box 349
   Thibodaux, LA 70302

MAINE

Bangor

Coca-Cola Bottling Company of
  Bangor
96 13th Street 04401

Farmington

Farmington Coca-Cola Bottling &
  Distributing Company, Inc.
1000 Lower Main Street
Box 2038 04938
207/778-4733

Lewiston

Coca-Cola Bottling Company of
  Lewiston
1750 Lisbon Street 04240

South Portland

The Coca-Cola Bottling Company
  of Northern New England, Inc.
316 Western Avenue 04106
207/773-5505

MARYLAND

Annapolis

Coca-Cola Bottling Company of
  Annapolis, Maryland, Inc.
2556 Riva Road 21401-7474
301/266-7840

Baltimore

Mid-Atlantic Coca-Cola Bottling
  Company, Inc.
700-1 North Kresson Street 21205
301/327-7505

Mid-Atlantic Coca-Cola Bottling
  Company, Inc.
2012 Hammonds Ferry Road 21227

Cambridge

Coca-Cola Bottling Company of
  Cambridge, Maryland, Inc.
211 Washington Street 21613
Mailing address: P.O. Box 273
  Cambridge, MD 21613
301/228-3232

Cumberland

Central Coca-Cola Bottling
  Company, Inc.
Highlands Sales Center
312 Greene Street 21502-0442

Frederick

Mid-Atlantic Coca-Cola Bottling
  Company, Inc.
1705 North Market Street 21701

Hagerstown

Central Coca-Cola Bottling
  Company, Inc.
Hagerstown Production Center
100 Charles Street 21740-3799

Havre de Grace

Mid-Atlantic Coca-Cola
  Bottling Co.
Havre de Grace Sales Center
315 Juniata Street 21078

La Plata

Mid-Atlantic Coca-Cola Bottling
  Co.
La Plata Sales Center
400 East Charles Street 20646
Mailing address: P.O. Box 686
  La Plata, MD 20646

Salisbury

Mid-Atlantic Coca-Cola
  Bottling Co.
Salisbury Sales & Production
  Center
410 Railroad Avenue 21801
Mailing address: P.O. Box 1718
  Salisbury, MD 21801

Silver Spring

Mid-Atlantic Coca-Cola Bottling
  Company, Inc.
1710 Elton Road 20903
301/439-7100

Westminster

Westminster Coca-Cola Bottling
  Company, Inc.
525 Old Westminster Pike 21157
Mailing address: P.O. Box 519
  Westminster, MD 21157
301/848-5680

MASSACHUSETTS

Braintree

Coca-Cola Bottling Company of
  New England
825 Granite Street 02185

Fall River

Coca-Cola Bottling Company of
  New England
1244 Davol Street 02722

Greenfield

Coca-Cola Bottling Company of
  Northampton
180 Silvio Conte Drive 01301
Mailing address: One Roundhouse
  Plaza
  Northampton, MA 01060
413/582-1400

Lowell

Coca-Cola Bottling Company of
  Lowell
160 Industrial Avenue, East 01853

Lynn

Coca-Cola Bottling Company of
  New England
654 Chestnut Street 01904

Needham Heights

Coca-Cola Bottling Company of
  New England
9 "B" Street 02194
617/449-4300

Pittsfield

Coca-Cola Bottling Company of
  Northampton
15 Commercial Street 01201
Mailing address: P.O. Box 1532
  Pittsfield, MA 01201

Sandwich

Coca-Cola Bottling Company of
  Cape Cod, Inc.
370 Route 130 02563
Mailing address: P.O. Box 779
  Sandwich, MA 02563
508/888-0001

MICHIGAN

Alpena

Coca-Cola Bottling Company of
  Michigan
171 North Industrial Highway
  49707

Bay City

Coca-Cola Bottling Company of
  Michigan
2500 Broadway 48707
Mailing address: P.O. Box 798
  Bay City, MI 48706

Cadillac

Coca-Cola Bottling Company of
  Michigan
U.S. 131 South 49601
Mailing address: P.O. Box 117
  Cadillac, MI 49601

Coldwater

Coca-Cola Bottling Company of
  Michigan
400 Race Street 49036
Mailing address: P.O. Box 137
  Coldwater, MI 49036

Detroit

Coca-Cola Bottlers of Detroit, Inc.
5981 West Warren Avenue 48210
313/897-5000

Escanaba

Bink's Coca-Cola Bottling
  Company
3001 Danforth Road 49829
906/786-4144

Flint

Coca-Cola Bottling Company of
  Michigan
2515 Lapeer Road 48503
313/234-4608

Grand Rapids

Coca-Cola Bottling Company of
  Michigan
1440 Butterworth St., S.W. 49504
Mailing address: P.O. Box 830
  Grand Rapids, MI 49508
616/942-8380

Coca-Cola Bottling Company of
  Michigan
3741 Patterson Avenue 49508
Mailing address: P.O. Box 830
  Grand Rapids, MI 49508

Hancock

Hancock Bottling Company, Inc.
1800 Birch Street 49930
906/482-3701

Jackson

Coca-Cola Bottling Company of
  Michigan
1610 Northwest Avenue 49202

Kalamazoo

Coca-Cola Bottling Company of
  Michigan
216 Peekstok Road 49001

Lansing

Coca-Cola Bottling Company of
  Michigan
3300 South Creyts Road 48917

Marquette

Coca-Cola Bottling Midwest, Inc.
950 West Washington Street 49855

Mt. Pleasant

Coca-Cola Bottling Company of
  Mt. Pleasant
808 South Adams 48858

Muskegon

Coca-Cola Bottling Company
1770 East Keating Avenue 49442

Petoskey

Coca-Cola Bottling Company of
    Michigan
1884 Harbor Springs Road 49770

St. Joseph

Great Lakes Coca-Cola Btlg Co.
200 Hawthorne Avenue 49085
Mailing address: P.O. Box 121
    St. Joseph, MI 49085

Traverse City

Coca-Cola Bottling Company of
    Michigan
1031 Hastings Street 49684

West Branch

Coca-Cola Bottling Company of
    Michigan
221 North Thomas 48661

MINNESOTA

Alexandria

Viking Coca-Cola Bottling
    Company
106 12th Avenue, West 56308
Mailing address: P.O. Box 909
    Alexandria, MN 56308

Bemidji

Coca-Cola Bottling Company of
    Bemidji, Inc.
116 Third Street 56601
218/751-1617

Crookston

Crookston Coca-Cola Bottling
    Company
609 Marin Avenue 56716
Mailing address: P.O. Box 55
    Crookston, MN 56716

Fergus Falls

Coca-Cola Bottling
    Fergus Falls, Inc.
832 Industrial Park Boulevard
    56537
218/736-5661

Hutchinson

Coca-Cola Bottling Company, Inc.
Highway 15 South 55350
Mailing address: P.O. Box 69
    Hutchinson, MN 55350

Marshall

Coca-Cola Bottling Company, Inc.
407 East Main Street 56258
Mailing address: P.O. Box 619
    Marshall, MN 56258-0619
507/532-4486

Moorhead

Coca-Cola Bottling Company
    Midwest, Inc.
2000 1st Avenue North 56560

Pine City

Coca-Cola Bottling Company of
    Pine City, Inc.
30 Sixth Street 55063
Mailing address: P.O. Box 169
    Pine City, MN 55063

Red Wing

Coca-Cola Bottling Company of
  Red Wing, Inc.
316 Bluff Street 55066
Mailing address: P.O. Box 418
  Red Wing, MN 55066
612/388-4012

St. Paul

Coca-Cola Bottling Midwest
  Company
2750 Eagandale Boulevard 55121
Mailing address: P.O. Box 64268
  St. Paul, MN 55164
612/454-5460

Willmar

Viking Coca-Cola Bottling
  Company
Hwy 12 West 56201
Mailing address: P.O. Box 411
  Willmar, MN 56201

Winona

Coca-Cola Bottling Company of
  Winona
102 Franklin Street 55987
507/452-2760

MISSISSIPPI

Clarksdale

Coca-Cola Bottling Company of
  Mississippi
320 Anderson Boulevard 38614
Mailing address: P.O. Box 519
  Clarksdale, MS 38614

Corinth

Corinth Coca-Cola Bottling Works,
  Inc.
601 Washington Street 38834
Mailing address: P.O. Box 229
  Corinth, MS 38834
601/287-1433

Greenwood

Jackson Coca-Cola Bottling
  Company
  Greenwood Branch
1000 West Park Avenue 38930
Mailing address: P.O. Box 1197
  Greenwood, MS 38930

Gulfport

Coast Coca-Cola Bottling
  Company, Inc.
3701 25th Avenue 39501
Mailing address: P.O. Drawer E
  Gulfport, MS 39502
601/864-1122

Jackson

Jackson Coca-Cola Bottling
  Company
1421 Highway 80 West 39204
Mailing address: P.O. Box 2397
  Jackson, MS 39205-2397
601/355-6487

Laurel

Laurel Coca-Cola Bottling
  Company
904 Ellisville Blvd. 39440
Mailing address: P.O. Box 2365
  Laurel, MS 39440
601/428-0464

McComb

Coca-Cola Bottling Company
  McComb Sales Center
Highway 24 South 39648
Mailing address: P.O. Box 568
  McComb, MS 39648

Meridian

Meridian Coca-Cola Bottling
  Company
2016 Highway 45 North 39301
Mailing address: P.O. Box 5207
  Meridian, MS 39301
601/483-5272

Natchez

Natchez Coca-Cola Bottling
  Company, Inc.
191 Deveraux Drive 39120
Mailing address: P.O. Box 885
  Natchez, MS 39120

Sardis

Coca-Cola & Dr. Pepper Bottling
  Co.
Access Road
Industrial Park 38666
Mailing address: P.O. Box 156
  Sardis, MS 38666

Vicksburg

Coca-Cola Bottling Company, Inc.
  of Vicksburg
2133 Washington Street 39180
Mailing address: P.O. Box 311
  Vicksburg, MS 39180

MISSOURI

Bolivar

Ozarks Coca-Cola & Dr. Pepper
  Bottling Company
912 West Broadway 65613
Mailing address: P.O. Box 522
  Bolivar, MO 65613

Flat River

Coca-Cola Bottling Company of
  Flat River
607 Buckley Street 63601

Jackson

Coca-Cola Bottling Company of
  Southeast Missouri
1125 Lenco Avenue 63755
Mailing address: P.O. Box 307
  Jackson, MO 63755
314/243-3131

Jefferson City

Jefferson City Coca-Cola Bottling
  Company
604 Jefferson Street 65101
314/636-6165

Joplin

Joplin Coca-Cola Bottling Company
1301 Virginia 64801

Kennett

Coca-Cola Bottling Company of
  Kennett
128 South By-Pass 63857
314/888-4767

Lebanon

Lebanon Coca-Cola Bottling
  Company
503 West Elm Street 65536
Mailing address: P.O. Box 71
  Lebanon, MO 65536

Maryland Heights

Coca-Cola Bottling Company of St.
  Louis
19 Worthington Drive 63043
314/878-0800

Poplar Bluff

Coca-Cola Bottling Company of
  Poplar Bluff
420 Pine 63901

Rolla

Ozarks Coca-Cola & Dr. Pepper
  Bottling Company - Rolla
  Division
Hypoint Industrial Park 65401
Mailing address: P.O. Box 787
  Rolla, MO 65401

Sedalia

Coca-Cola Bottling Company of
  Mid-America
813 West 16th Street 65301

Springfield

Ozarks Coca-Cola & Dr. Pepper
  Bottling Company
1777 North Packer Road 65803
Mailing address: P.O. Box 11250
  Springfield, MO 65808-1250
417/865-9900

West Plains

West Plains Coca-Cola Bottling
  Company
218 West Broadway 65775
Mailing address: P.O. Box 370
  Jonesboro, AR 72403

MONTANA

Billings

Coca-Cola Bottling Co. West, Inc.
4151 First Avenue South 59101
406/245-6211

Glasgow

Coca-Cola Bottling Company of
  Glasgow
109 Second Street, South 59230
406/228-4541

Glendive

Glendive Coca-Cola Bottling
  Company, Inc.
220 South Douglas 59330
Mailing address: P.O. Box 1049
  Glendive, MT 59330
406/365-3750

Great Falls

Coca-Cola Bottling Company West
933 38th Street, North 59401
Mailing address: P.O. Box 7038
  Great Falls, MT 59406
406/761-3794

Helena

Lehrkind's Helena Coca-Cola
  Bottling Company
1698 "A" Street 59604
Mailing address: P.O. Box 4147
  Helena, MT 59604

Kalispell

Coca-Cola Bottling Company
Kalispell Sales Center
451 North Main Street 59901

Miles City

Coca-Cola Bottling Company
1620 Palmer 59301

Missoula

Coca-Cola Bottling Company, West
2010 South Third Street, West
59801
406/549-4132

NEBRASKA

Chadron

National Drinks, Inc.
P.O. Box 206 69337

Grand Island

Grand Island Bottling Company
1617 South Holland Drive 68802

Kearney

Coca-Cola & Dr. Pepper Bottling
Company
119 West Railroad Street 68847
Mailing address: P.O. Box 398
Kearney, NE 68847

Lincoln

Wichita Coca-Cola Bottling
Company
2120 "G" Street 68510
Mailing address: P.O. Box 30265
Lincoln, NE 68510
402/475-3749

Nebraska City

Nebraska City Coca-Cola Bottling
Co.
213 Central Avenue 68410
Mailing address: P.O. Box 459
Nebraska City, NE 68410

Norfolk

Norfolk Coca-Cola Bottling
Company
P.O. Box 1143 68701

Omaha

Coca-Cola Bottling Company of
Mid-America
3200 North 30th Street 68111

Scottsbluff

National Drinks, Inc.
2022 East 17th Street 69361

NEVADA

Las Vegas

Coca-Cola Bottling Company
424 North Main Street 89101

NEW HAMPSHIRE

Claremont

Coca-Cola Bottling Company of
  Claremont
285 Main Street 03743
Mailing address: P.O. Box 828
  Claremont, NH 03743

Laconia

CC Vending, Inc.
128 Messer Street 03246

Manchester

Coca-Cola Bottling Company of
  Manchester
99 Eddy Road 03102

Salem

Coca-Cola Bottling Company of
  Salem
23 South Broadway 03079
Mailing address: P.O. Box 25
  Salem, NH 03079

NEW JERSEY

Moorestown

Coca-Cola Bottling Company of
  South Jersey
1250 Glen Avenue 08057
Mailing address: P.O. Box 186
  Moorestown, NJ 08057
609/235-7758

North Brunswick

The Coca-Cola Bottling Company
  of New York
1500 Livingston Avenue 08902

Paterson

The Coca-Cola Bottling Company
  of New York, Inc.
263 McLean Boulevard 07504
201/684-0037

NEW MEXICO

Albuquerque

The Coca-Cola & Dr. Pepper
  Bottling Company of
  Albuquerque
205 Marquette Avenue, NE 87102
Mailing address: P.O. Box 25486
  Albuquerque, NM 87125
505/243-2811

Carlsbad

Southwest Coca-Cola Bottling
  Company
602 South Canal 88220
Mailing address: P.O. Box C
  Carlsbad, NM 88220

Clovis

Southwest Coca-Cola Bottling
  Company
2800 West 7th Street 88101

Deming

Deming Coca-Cola Bottling
  Company
2401 Atlantic Way 88031
Mailing address: P.O. Box 750
  Deming, NM 88031-0750
505/546-9331

Farmington

Durango Coca-Cola Bottling
  Company
105 East Maple Avenue 87401

Gallup

Coca-Cola & Dr. Pepper Bottling
    Company of Gallup, Inc.
2522 East 66th Avenue 87301
Mailing address: P.O. Box 98
    Gallup, NM 87031

Hobbs

Southwest Coca-Cola Bottling Co.
1203 East Broadway 88240

Las Cruces

Las Cruces Coca-Cola Bottling
    Company
2100 South Valley Drive 88001
Mailing address: P.O. Box 729
    Las Cruces, NM 88004
505/526-5534

Santa Fe

Coca-Cola Bottling Company of
    Santa Fe, Inc.
660 West San Mateo Road 87501
Mailing address: P.O. Drawer K
    Santa Fe, NM 87504-0288
505/983-4612

NEW YORK

Albany

The Coca-Cola Bottling Company
    of New York, Inc.
38 Warehouse Row 12205
Mailing address: P.O. Box 5268
    Albany, NY 12205

Binghamton

Binghamton Coca-Cola Bottling
    Company
Seven Walter Avenue 13901

Bronx

The Coca-Cola Bottling Company
    of New York
977 East 149th Street 10455

Dansville

Coca-Cola Bottling Company
North Main Street 14437
Mailing address: P.O. Box 36
    Dansville, NY 14437

Elmsford

The Coca-Cola Bottling Company
    of New York, Inc.
111 Fairview Park Drive 10523
914/592-4574

Hauppauge, L.I.

The Coca-Cola Bottling Company
    of New York
1765 Express Drive, North 11787

Horseheads

Elmira Coca-Cola Bottling
    Company
Latta Brook Park 14845
Mailing address: P.O. Box 310
    Horseheads, NY 14845

Maspeth

The Coca-Cola Bottling Company
    of New York, Inc.
59-02 Borden Avenue 11378
718/326-3334

New Windsor

The Coca-Cola Bottling Company
    of New York
10 Hempstead Road 12550

Plattsburgh

Plattsburgh Coca-Cola Bottling
  Company, Inc.
Beekmantown Road 12901
Mailing address: P.O. Box 690
  Plattsburgh, NY 12901

Seneca Falls

Finger Lakes Coca-Cola Bottling
  Company
P.O. Box 325 13148

Syracuse

The Coca-Cola Bottling Company
  of New York, Inc.
Farrell Road & John Glenn Blvd.
  13221
Mailing address: P.O. Box 4882
  Syracuse, NY 13221

Tonawanda

Coca-Cola Bottling Company of
  Buffalo
200 Milens Road 14150

NORTH CAROLINA

Aberdeen

Aberdeen Coca-Cola Bottling
  Company
203 West South Street 28315
Mailing address: P.O. Box 518
  Aberdeen, NC 28315
919/944-2305

Albemarle

Albemarle Coca-Cola Bottling
  Company
1610 East Main Street 28001
Mailing address: P.O. Box 69
  Albemarle, NC 28001

Biscoe

Biscoe Coca-Cola Bottling
  Company, Inc.
315 South Main Street 27209
Mailing address: P.O. Box 189
  Biscoe, NC 27209
919/428-2155

Boone

Coca-Cola Bottling Company
105 By-Pass 28607
Mailing address: P.O. Box 1099
  Boone, NC 28607

Burlington

Burlington Coca-Cola Bottling
  Company
825 South Main Street 27215
Mailing address: P.O. Box 479
  Burlington, NC 27215

Charlotte

Coca-Cola Bottling Co.
  Consolidated
  Snyder Production Center
4901 Chesapeake Drive 28216
Mailing address: P.O. Box 31487
  Charlotte, NC 28231
704/393-4200

Coca-Cola Bottling Company
  Consolidated
1900 Rexford Road 28211
Mailing address: P.O. Box 31487
  Charlotte, NC 28231
704/551-4400

Durham

Durham Coca-Cola Bottling
  Company
3214 Hillsborough Road 27705
Mailing address: P.O. Box 2627
  Durham, NC 27705
919/383-1531

Elizabeth City

Mid-Atlantic Coca-Cola Bottling
   Company, Inc.
521 West Broad Street 27909

Fayetteville

Fayetteville Coca-Cola Bottling
   Company
1225 Ramsey Street 28302
Mailing address: P.O. Box 1180
   Fayetteville, NC 28301
919/483-6158

Forest City

Coca-Cola Bottling Company
752 East Main Street 28043
Mailing address: P.O. Box 150
   Forest City, NC 28043

Gastonia

Choice U.S.A. Beverage, Inc.
620 West Franklin Blvd. 28052
Mailing address: P.O. Box 2669
   Gastonia, NC 28053
704/865-1279

Goldsboro

Eastern Carolina Coca-Cola
   Bottling Company, Inc.
701 South George Street 27530
Mailing Address: P.O. Box 24
   Goldsboro, NC 27530
919/735-2653

Hamlet

Hamlet Coca-Cola Bottling
   Company
Highway 74 East 28345
Mailing address: P.O. Box 711
   Hamlet, NC 28345

Henderson

Coca-Cola Bottling Company
   of Henderson, Inc.
U.S. #1 South Raleigh Road 27536
Mailing address: P.O. Box 378
   Henderson, NC 27536
919/438-5114

Hickory

Coca-Cola Bottling Company
820 First Avenue, Northwest 28601
Mailing address: P.O. Box 1119
   Hickory, NC 28601

Kinston

Kinston Coca-Cola
   Bottling Company, Inc.
Highway 70 West 28501
Mailing address: P.O. Box 337
   Kinston, NC 28501

Lumberton

Fayetteville Coca-Cola Bottling Co.
   Lumberton Branch
500 East First Street 28358

Morganton

Coca-Cola Bottling Company
1500 East Union Street 28655
704/433-5190

New Bern

New Bern Coca-Cola
    Bottling Works, Inc.
Highway 17 28560
Mailing address: P.O. Drawer D
New Bern, NC 28560

Plymouth

Plymouth Coca-Cola
    Bottling Company, Inc.
111 East Water Street 27962

Raleigh

Capital Coca-Cola Bottling
    Company
2200 South Wilmington Street
    27611
Mailing address: P.O. Box 26748
    Raleigh, NC 27611
919/834-2551

Rocky Mount

Coca-Cola Bottling Company of
    Rocky Mount, Inc.
442 South Church Street 27801
Mailing address: P.O. Box 832
    Rocky Mount, NC 27802-0832

Salisbury

Coca-Cola Bottling Company of
    Salisbury
1828 South Main Street 28144
Mailing address: P.O. Box 607
    Salisbury, NC 28144

Sanford

Sanford Coca-Cola Bottling
    Company
1605 Hawkins Avenue 27330
Mailing address: P.O. Drawer 1207
    Sanford, NC 27330
919/774-4111

Shelby

Coca-Cola Bottling Company of
    Shelby
925 East Marion Street 28150
Mailing address: P.O. Box 789
    Shelby, NC 28150

Statesville

Coca-Cola Bottling Company of
    Statesville
2027 West Front Street 28677
Mailing address: P.O. Box 5360
    Statesville, NC 28677

Tarboro

Tarboro Coca-Cola Bottling
    Company, Inc.
1406 Main Street 27886
Mailing address: P.O. Box 399
    Tarboro, NC 27886

Washington

Coca-Cola Bottling Company of
    Washington, NC, Inc.
905 West Fifth Street 27889
Mailing address: P.O. Box 940
    Washington, NC 27889
919/946-6106

Weldon

Weldon Coca-Cola Bottling Works,
    Inc.
10 East Sycamore Street 27890
919/536-3611

Wilmington

Wilmington Coca-Cola Bottling
    Works, Inc.
918 Princess Street 28401
919/762-0375

Wilson

Fayetteville Coca-Cola Bottling Co.
  Wilson Branch
2612 Wilco Boulevard South
  27893
Mailing address: P.O. Box 665
  Wilson, NC 27894-0665

Winston-Salem

Winston-Salem Coca-Cola Bottling
  Company
730 South Marshall Street 27108
Mailing address: P.O. 10549
  Winston-Salem 27108

NORTH DAKOTA

Bismarck

Coca-Cola Bottling Co. West, Inc.
3225 East Thayer 58501
701/222-1200

Grand Forks

Grand Forks Coca-Cola Bottling
  Company
714–724 North 47th Street 58201
Mailing address: P.O. 578
  Grand Forks, ND 58201

OHIO

Akron

The Coca-Cola Bottling Company
  of Ohio
1560 Triplett Boulevard 44306
216/784-2653

Canton

Cameron Coca-Cola Bottling
  Company
4922 Navarre Road, S.W. 44706

Cincinnati

Coca-Cola Bottling Company of
  Cincinnati
5100 Duck Creek Road 45227-
  1489
513/527-6600

Circleville

Scioto Coca-Cola Bottling
  Company
450 East Town Street 43113
Mailing address: P.O. Box 454
  Circleville, OH 43113
614/474-2189

Cleveland

Cleveland Coca-Cola Bottling
  Company
3705 Carnegie Avenue 44115
216/391-7665

Columbus

Coca-Cola Bottling Company of
  Ohio
786 Twin Rivers Drive 43212

Dayton

The Dayton Coca-Cola Bottling
  Company
901 South Ludlow Street 45402

Elyria

The Elyria Coca-Cola Bottling
  Company
1410 Lake Avenue 44035

Findlay

Findlay Coca-Cola, Inc.
122 Clinton Court 45840

Lima

Lima Coca-Cola Bottling Co., Inc.
201 North Shore Drive 45802-
0746

Marion

Coca-Cola Bottling Company
309 North Main Street 43302

Mentor

The Painesville Coca-Cola Bottling
Company
8755 Munson Road 44060
Mailing address: P.O. Box 423
Mentor, OH 44060

Newark

Mid-Ohio Coca-Cola Bottling
Company, Inc.
250 East Main Street 43055
Mailing address: P.O. Box 820
Newark, OH 43055

Portsmouth

Mid-Atlantic Coca-Cola Bottling
Company, Inc.
3001 Scioto Trail 45662

Steubenville

Cameron Coca-Cola Bottling
Company, Inc.
813 Stoney Hollow Boulevard
43952

Toledo

Coca-Cola Bottling Company of
Ohio
3970 Catawba Street 43612
Mailing address: P.O. Box 6818
Toledo, OH 43612

Youngstown

The Coca-Cola Bottling Company
of Ohio
531 East Indianola Avenue 44502

Zanesville

The Zanesvile Coca-Cola Bottling
Company
Seventh & Harvey Streets 43701
Mailing address: P.O. Box 150
Zanesville, OH 43701

OKLAHOMA

Altus

Southwest Coca-Cola Bottling Co.
601 Todd Lane 73521

Alva

Alva Coca-Cola Bottling Company,
Inc.
114 Flynn Avenue 73717
Mailing address: P.O. Box 724
Alva, OK 73717

Clinton

Southwest Coca-Cola Bottling Co.
2310 Corbin Lane 73601

Idabel

Idabel Coca-Cola Bottling
Company, Inc.
500 South Central Avenue 74745
Mailing address: P.O. Box 237
Idabel, OK 74745
405/286-2653

Lawton

Southwest Coca-Cola Bottling Co.
511 North West Second Street
73501

Oklahoma City

Great Plains Coca-Cola Bottling
  Company
600 North May Avenue 73107
Mailing address: P.O. Box 75220
  Oklahoma City, OK 73147
405/943-8311

Okmulgee

Great Plains Coca-Cola Bottling
  Co.
1304 West 20th Street 74447
Mailing address: P.O. Drawer 1367
  Okmulgee, OK 74447
918/756-9050

Vinita

Great Plains Coca-Cola Bottling
  Company
State Hospital Road 74301
Mailing address: P.O. Box 927
  Vinita, OK 74301

Woodward

Woodward Coca-Cola Bottling
  Company
Ninth & Santa Fe Streets 73801

OREGON

John Day

Gardner Enterprises, Inc.
195 Northeast Second Avenue
  97845
503/575-1410

Klamath Falls

Coca-Cola Bottling Company of
  Klamath Falls
105 North Spring Street 97601

Medford

Medford Coca-Cola Bottling
  Company
3074 Crater Lake Avenue 97501

North Bend

Coca-Cola Bottling Company of
  Oregon
860 Florida Street 97429

Pendleton

Coca-Cola Bottling Company of
  Pendleton
410 Southeast Fourth Street 97801
Mailing address: P.O. Box 1007
  Pendleton, OR 97801

Portland

Coca-Cola Bottling Company of
  Oregon
3599 Northwest Yeon Avenue
  97210

Salem

Pacific Coca-Cola Bottling
  Company
1220 South 12th Street, S.E. 97302

The Dalles

Coca-Cola Bottling Company of
  Oregon
2100 West Second 97058

Wilsonville

Coca-Cola Bottling Company of
  Oregon
9750 Southwest Barbur Street
  97070
503/248-1064

PENNSYLVANIA

Bethlehem

Coca-Cola Bottling Company of
the Lehigh Valley
2150 Industrial Drive 18001
215/866-8020

Coatesville

Coatesville Coca-Cola Bottling
Works, Inc.
174 North Caln Road 19320
215/384-4343

DuBois

Coca-Cola Bottling Company of
DuBois, Inc.
601 East DuBois Avenue 15801
Mailing address: P.O. Box 387
DuBois, PA 15801

Ebensburg

Consolidated Coca-Cola Bottling
Company
Route 422 West 15931
814/472-6112

Erie

Erie Coca-Cola Bottling Company
2209 West 50th Street 16509
Mailing address: P.O. Box 10237
Erie, PA 16514
814/833-0101

Greensburg

Greensburg Coca-Cola Bottling
Company, Inc.
501 West Otterman Street 15601

Lancaster

Mid-Atlantic Coca-Cola Bottling
Company, Inc.
1428 Manheim Pike 17604
Mailing address: P.O. Box 4103
Lancaster, PA 17604

Meadville

Coca-Cola Bottling Company of
Meadville
421 North Street 16335

Philadelphia

The Philadelphia Coca-Cola
Bottling Company
Erie Avenue & "G" Street 19134
215/427-4500

Phoenixville

Superior Beverage Company
1–11 North Main Street 19460
Mailing address: P.O. Box 547
Phoenixville, PA 19460
215/933-5881

Pittston

Keystone Coca-Cola Bottling
Company
300 Oak Street 18640
717/655-2874

Pottsville

Coca-Cola Bottling Company of
Pottsville
2200 West Market Street 17901
717/622-6991

Reading

Reading Coca-Cola Bottling Works,
Inc.
Madison Avenue & Bern Street
19603

Shiremanstown

Mid-Atlantic Coca-Cola Bottling
Company, Inc.
4825 Old Gettysburg Road 17011
Mailing address: P.O. Box 126
Shiremanstown, PA 17011

Sunbury

Mid-Atlantic Coca-Cola Bottling
Company, Inc.
200 North River Avenue 17801
Mailing address: P.O. Box 245
Sunbury, PA 17801

Uniontown

Coca-Cola Bottling Company of
Uniontown
244 Pittsburgh Street 15401

Washington

Cameron Coca-Cola Bottling
Company, Inc.
124 West Maiden Street 15301
Mailing address: P.O. Box 814
Washington, PA 15301
412/222-7700

Williamsport

Williamsport Coca-Cola Bottling
Company, Inc.
1350 Washington Boulevard 17701

York

York Coca-Cola Bottling Co., Inc.
2611 East Market Street 17402-
1543

RHODE ISLAND

Providence

Coca-Cola Bottling Company of
New England
95 Pleasant Valley Parkway 02901
Mailing address: P.O. Box 696
Providence, RI 02901

SOUTH CAROLINA

Aiken

Columbia Coca-Cola Bottling Co.
Aiken Sales Center
621 York Street, N.E. 29801
Mailing address: P.O. Drawer C
Aiken, SC 29801

Anderson

Coca-Cola Bottling Company of
Anderson
440–442 East Orr Street 29621
Mailing address: P.O. Box 766
Anderson, SC 29621

Charleston

Charleston Coca-Cola Bottling
Company, Inc.
823 Meeting Street 29403
Mailing address: P.O. Box 6218
Charleston, SC 29405

Columbia

Columbia Coca-Cola Bottling
Company
2830 Main Street 29202
Mailing address: P.O. Drawer 31
Columbia, SC 29202
803/779-3580

Conway

Coastal Coca-Cola Bottling
  Company
Highway 501 By-Pass 29526
Mailing address: P.O. Box 376
  Conway, SC 29526

Florence

Coastal Coca-Cola Bottling
  Company
Pisgah Road (Off Highway 52)
  29503
Mailing address: P.O. Box 146
  Florence, SC 29503

Greenville

Coca-Cola Bottling Company of
  Greenville
516 Buncombe Street 29603
Mailing address: P.O. Box 2528
  Greenville, SC 29603

Hampton

Hampton Coca-Cola Bottling
  Works
100 Lightsey Street 29924
Mailing address: P.O. Box 276
  Hampton, SC 29924

Marion

Coastal Coca-Cola Bottling
  Company
Coleman Curve Road 29571
Mailing address: P.O. Drawer 1029
  Marion, SC 29571
803/423-4734

Rock Hill

Rock Hill Coca-Cola Bottling
  Company
520 North Cherry Road 29730
Mailing address: P.O. Box 2555
  Rock Hill, SC 29730
803/328-2406

Spartanburg

Coca-Cola Bottling Company
  Spartanburg Sales Center
500 West Main Street 29301
Mailing address: P.O. Box 1012
  Spartanburg, SC 29304

Summerville

Dorchester Coca-Cola Bottling
  Company
118 South Cedar Street 29483

SOUTH DAKOTA

Aberdeen

Coca-Cola Bottling Company of
  Aberdeen, Inc.
221 North Main Street 57401
Mailing address: P.O. Box 38
  Aberdeen, SD 57402-0038
605/225-6780

Huron

Coca-Cola Bottling Company
227 Dakota Street, North 57350

Mitchell

Coca-Cola Bottling Company of
  Central South Dakota, Inc.
120 South Kimball Street 57301
Mailing address: P.O. Box 39
  Mitchell, SD 57301
605/996-5633

Mobridge

Coca-Cola Bottling Company
West Shore Acres 57601
Mailing address: P.O. Box 496
  Mobridge, SD 57601

Pierre

Coca-Cola Bottling Company
124 East Dakota Avenue 57501
Mailing address: P.O. Box 217
  Pierre, SD 57501

Rapid City

Coca-Cola Bottling Company of
  the Black Hills
2150 Coca-Cola Lane 57702
605/342-8222

Sioux Falls

Coca-Cola Bottling Company of
  Sioux Falls
2301 South Minnesota Avenue
  57105
Mailing address: P.O. Box 833
  Sioux Falls, SD 57101

Watertown

Coca-Cola Bottling Company
405 Cessna Street 57201

TENNESSEE

Brownsville

Coca-Cola Bottling Company of
  West Tennessee
1303 South Dupree Avenue 38012
Mailing address: P.O. Box 885
  Brownsville, TN 38012

Chattanooga

Chattanooga Coca-Cola Bottling
  Company
4000 Amnicola Highway 37406
Mailing address: P.O. Box 11128
  Chattanooga, TN 37401
615/624-4681

Cleveland

Johnston Coca-Cola Bottling
  Company
Highway 64 Bypass
Refreshment Lane 37311
Mailing address: P.O. Box 88
  Cleveland, TN 37311
615/476-1131

Columbia

Coca-Cola Bottling Works of
  Columbia
Nashville Highway 38401
Mailing address: P.O. Box 559
  Columbia, TN 38401-0559

Cookeville

Johnston Coca-Cola Bottling
  Company
434 West Spring Street 38501

Dickson

Coca-Cola Bottling Company of
  Dickson
101 Cowan Road 37055
Mailing address: P.O. Box 159
  Dickson, TN 37055

Dyersburg

Coca-Cola Bottling Company of
  Dyersburg, Inc.
531 East Cedar Street 38024

Jackson

Coca-Cola Bottling Works of
  Jackson, Inc.
457 Riverside Drive 38301
Mailing address: P.O. Box 1804
  Jackson, TN 38302-1804
901/424-2697

Johnson City

Johnson City Coca-Cola Bottling
  Co.
310 Wesley Street 37605
Mailing address: P.O. Drawer 1757
  Johnson City, TN 37605
615/282-2511

Knoxville

Roddy Coca-Cola Bottling
  Company
2200 Leslie Street 37921
Mailing address: P.O. Box 50338
  Knoxville, TN 37950-0338
615/546-6020

Lebanon

Coca-Cola Bottling Company of
  Lebanon
Highway 70 37088
Mailing address: P.O. Box 488
  Lebanon, TN 37088-0488

Lexington

Coca-Cola Bottling Works
10 Front Street 38351
Mailing address: P.O. Box 387
  Lexington, TN 38351

Memphis

Coca-Cola Bottling Company of
  Memphis
499 South Hollywood Street 38111
Mailing address: P.O. Box 11489
  Memphis, TN 38111
901/454-8700

Nashville

Coca-Cola Bottling Company of
  Nashville, Inc.
407 Craighead Street 37204
Mailing address: P.O. Box 40818
  Nashville, TN 37204
615/383-6230

Pulaski

Coca-Cola Bottling Works, Inc.
611 West College Street 38478
Mailing address: P.O. Box 269
  Pulaski, TN 38478
615/363-7443

Rockwood

Johnston Coca-Cola Bottling
  Company
220 South Kingston Avenue 37854
Mailing address: P.O. Box 207
  Rockwood, TN 37854

Springfield

Coca-Cola Bottling Company of
  Springfield
114 North Main Street 37172

Tullahoma

Coca-Cola Bottling Works of
  Tullahoma, Inc.
1502 E. Carroll Street 37388
Mailing address: P.O. Box 1750
  Tullahoma, TN 37388
615/455-3466

Union City

Union City Coca-Cola Bottling
   Company
1915 Reelfoot Avenue 38261
901/885-5140

TEXAS

Abilene

Southwest Coca-Cola Bottling Co.
2074 North First Street 79604
Mailing address: P.O. Box 1441
   Abilene, TX 79604
915/672-3232

Alpine

Big Bend Coca-Cola Bottling
   Company
West Highway 90 79830
Mailing address: P.O. Drawer 1650
   Alpine, TX 79830
915/837-2131

Amarillo

Southwest Coca-Cola Bottling Co.
701 South Lincoln 79105
Mailing address: P.O. Box 15050
   Amarillo, TX 79105
806/376-5421

Austin

Austin Coca-Cola Bottling
   Company
9600 Burnet Road 78758
Mailing address: P.O. Box 9140
   Austin, TX 78766
512/836-7272

Brownwood

San Angelo Coca-Cola Bottling Co.
1308 Center Avenue 76804
Mailing address: P.O. Box 1165
   Brownwood, TX 76804

Bryan

Bryan Coca-Cola Bottling Company
201 East 24th Street 77803
Mailing address: P.O. Drawer 433
   Bryan, TX 77806
409/823-8153

Childress

Wichita Coca-Cola Bottling
   Company
200 Second Street, N.E. 79201-
   0060
Mailing address: P.O. Box 60
   Childress, TX 79201-0060

Dalhart

Southwest Coca-Cola Bottling Co.
819 Chicago Avenue 79022
Mailing address: P.O. Box 391
   Dalhart, TX 79022

Dallas

Coca-Cola Bottling Company of
   North Texas
6011 Lemmon Avenue 75209
214/357-1781

El Paso

Magnolia Coca-Cola Bottling
   Company
11001 Gateway West 79935
Mailing address: P.O. Box 27000
   El Paso, TX 79926
915/593-2653

Fredericksburg

Austin Coca-Cola Bottling
  Company
425 West Main Street 78624

Graham

Coca-Cola Bottling Company of
  North Texas-Fort Worth
1040 East Fourth Street 76406
Mailing address: P.O. Box 756
  Graham, TX 76406

Houston

Houston Coca-Cola Bottling
  Company
2800 Bissonnet 77005
Mailing address: P.O. Box 1268
  Houston, TX 77251
713/664-3451

Houston Coca-Cola Bottling
  Company
2819 Berkley 77012
Mailing address: P.O. Box 1268
  Houston, TX 77001
713/641-3251

Laredo

The Laredo Coca-Cola Bottling
  Company, Inc.
1402 Industrial Boulevard 78041
512/726-2672

Longview

Longview Coca-Cola Bottling
  Company, Inc.
340 West Tyler Street 75601
Mailing address: P.O. Box 71
  Longview, TX 75606
214/753-7609

McAllen

Valley Coca-Cola Bottling
  Company
2400 Expressway 78502
Mailing address: P.O. Box 190
  McAllen, TX 78502
512/686-4311

Odessa

Southwest Coca-Cola Bottling Co.
2700 Van Street 79760

Paris

Paris Coca-Cola Bottling Company
1033 Bonham Street 75460

Pecos

Big Bend Coca-Cola Bottling
  Company
1101 Pinehurst 79772
Mailing address: P.O. Box 1364
  Pecos, TX 79772

Perryton

Perryton Coca-Cola Bottling
  Company, Inc.
1105 Highway 15 West 79070
806/435-4091

San Angelo

Coca-Cola Bottling Company
69 North Chadbourne Street 76903
Mailing address: P.O. Box 1192
  San Angelo, TX 76902
915/655-6991

San Antonio

Coca-Cola Bottling Company of
    the Southwest
#1 Coca-Cola Place 78219
Mailing address: P.O. Box 58
    San Antonio, TX 78291
512/225-2601

Sherman

Dallas Coca-Cola Bottling
    Company
Sherman Center
1820 Frisco Road 75090

Temple

Coca-Cola Bottling Company of
    the Southwest
1401 North Third Street 76501
Mailing address: P.O. Box 808
    Temple, TX 76503

Texarkana

Coca-Cola Bottling Company of
    Texarkana
1930 New Boston Road 75501
Mailing address: P.O. Box 5427
    Texarkana, TX 75505

Tyler

Dallas Coca-Cola Bottling
    Company
Tyler Center
3200 West Gentry Parkway 75202

Uvalde

Coca-Cola Bottling Company of
    the Southwest
301 South Getty Street 78801
Mailing address: P.O. Box 1548
    Uvalde, TX 78801

Victoria

Coca-Cola Bottling Company of
    the Southwest
4002 North Navarro 77901

Wichita Falls

Wichita Coca-Cola Bottling
    Company
1512 Lamar Street 76301
Mailing address: P.O. Box 5068
    Wichita Falls, TX 76307
817/766-3251

UTAH

Logan

Coca-Cola Bottling Company of
    Logan
975 West 800 North 84321

Provo

Coca-Cola Bottling Company of
    Provo
825 South Freedom Boulevard
    84601

Vernal

Coca-Cola Bottling Company of
    Vernal
760 North Vernal Avenue 84078
Mailing address: P.O. Box 96
    Provo, UT 84603
801/789-6535

VERMONT

Rutland

Coca-Cola Bottling Company of
    Northampton
One Quality Lane 05701
Mailing address: P.O. Box 387
    Rutland, VT 05701

VIRGINIA

Alexandria

Mid-Atlantic Coca-Cola Bottling
Company, Inc.
5401 Seminary Road 22311
Mailing address: P.O. Box 11245
Alexandria, VA 22311

Bristol

Coca-Cola Bottling Company of
Bristol
1913–35 West State Street 24203
Mailing address: P.O. Box 1119
Bristol, VA 24203-1119

Charlottesville

Charlottesville Coca-Cola Bottling
Company, Inc.
722 Preston Avenue 22906-6070

Clifton Forge

Coca-Cola Bottling Company of
Roanoke, Inc.
720 Main Street 24422
Mailing address: P.O. Box 607
Clifton Forge, VA 24422

Dublin

Coca-Cola Bottling Company of
Roanoke, Inc.
Route 100, S. Dublin 24084
Mailing address: P.O. Box 547
Dublin, VA 24084

Emporia

Emporia Coca-Cola Bottling
Company, Inc.
518 Halifax Street 23847
804/634-6161

Exmore

Mid-Atlantic Coca-Cola Bottling
Company, Inc.
Route #13 23350

Fredericksburg

Coca-Cola Bottling Company
2011 Princess Anne Street 22404

Harrisonburg

Harrisonburg Coca-Cola Bottling
Company
794 North Main Street 22801-4697

Lynchburg

Lynchburg Coca-Cola Bottling
Company, Inc.
3720 Abe Cohen Place 24506
Mailing address: P.O. Box 10157
Lynchburg, VA 24506
804/845-4595

Martinsville

Coca-Cola Bottling Company of
Roanoke, Inc.
1220 Memorial Boulevard, South
24112
Mailing address: P.O. Box 1108
Martinsville, VA 24112

Montross

Northern Neck Coca-Cola Bottling
Company, Inc.
Kings Highway & Rectory Road
22520
Mailing address: P.O. Box 325
Montross, VA 22520
804/493-8051

Norfolk

Mid-Atlantic Coca-Cola Bottling
  Company, Inc.
2000 Monticello Avenue 23517
Mailing address: P.O. Box 11186
  Norfolk, VA 23517

Roanoke

Coca-Cola Bottling Company of
  Roanoke, Inc.
235 Shenandoah Avenue, N.W.
  24016
703/343-8041

South Boston

Coca-Cola Bottling Company of
  Roanoke, Inc.
Highway 58, West 24592
Mailing address: P.O. Box 306
  South Boston, VA 24592

Staunton

Staunton Coca-Cola Bottling
  Company, Inc.
Road 647, Route 11 South 24401-
  1033
Mailing address: P.O. Box 2216
  Staunton, VA 24401-1033
703/886-3427

Suffolk

Mid-Atlantic Coca-Cola Bottling
  Company, Inc.
1390 Progress Road 23434

Winchester

Winchester Coca-Cola Bottling
  Company, Inc.
1720 Valley Avenue 22601-0382
Mailing address: P.O. Box 3174
  Winchester, VA 22601-0382

WASHINGTON

Bellevue

Pacific Coca-Cola Bottling
  Company
1150 124th Avenue, N.E. 98009
Mailing address: P.O. Box C-03346
  Bellevue, WA 98009
206/455-2000

Bellingham

Coca-Cola Bottling Company of
  Bellingham
2101 Woburn Street 98225
Mailing address: P.O. Box 98
  Bellingham, WA 98225
206/734-6130

Marysville

Pacific Coca-Cola Bottling
  Company
7610 - 47th Avenue, Northeast
  98270

Spokane

Pacific Coca-Cola Bottling
  Company
North 901 Monroe Street 99201

Tacoma

Pacific Coca-Cola Bottling
  Company
3333 South 38th Street 98409
Mailing address: P.O. Box 11025
  Tacoma, WA 98411

Wenatchee

Coca-Cola Bottling Company of
  Wenatchee
16 North Columbia Street 98801
Mailing address: P.O. Box 189
  Wenatchee, WA 98801

WEST VIRGINIA

Beckley

Coca-Cola Bottling Company of
  Beckley, Inc.
700 South Oakwood Avenue 25801

Bluefield

Coca-Cola Bottling Company of
  Bluefield
Pinnacle View Road 24701

Charleston

Coca-Cola Bottling Works of
  Charleston, Inc.
3211 MacCorkle Avenue, S.E.
  25304

Fairmont

Fairmont Coca-Cola Bottling
  Company, Inc.
Highlands Sales Center
1200 Morgantown Avenue
26554-1736

Huntington

Coca-Cola Bottling Company of
  Huntington
401 Third Avenue 25701
Mailing address: P.O. Box 1238
  Huntington, WV 25714

Parkersburg

Coca-Cola Bottling Company of
  Parkersburg
1600 13th Street 26101

WISCONSIN

Beaver Dam

Coca-Cola Bottling Co. of
  Wisconsin
  Beaver Dam Sales Center
520 East Burnett Street 53916

Eau Claire

Midwest Coca-Cola Bottling
  Company
623 Hastings Way 54701

Green Bay

Coca-Cola Bottling Company of
  Wisconsin
  Green Bay Sales Center
2523 South Oneida Street 54305

Kenosha

Coca-Cola Bottling Co. of Chicago
  Kenosha Sales Center
5017 Sheridan Road 53140
Mailing address: P.O. Box 767
  Kenosha, WI 53140

Madison

Coca-Cola Bottling Company of
  Mid-America
3536 University Avenue 53705

Milwaukee

Coca-Cola Bottling Co. of
  Wisconsin
  Milwaukee Sales Center
2727 West Silver Spring Drive
  53209

Oshkosh

Coca-Cola Bottling Co. of
  Wisconsin
  Oshkosh Sales Center
1404 South Main Street 54901
Mailing address: P.O. Box 2097
  Oshkosh, WI 54903

Rhinelander

Coca-Cola Bottling Company, Inc.
415 Iverson Street 54501
Mailing address: P.O. Box 1108
  Rhinelander, WI 54501

Rice Lake

St. Croix Valley Coca-Cola Bottling
  Company
326 South Main Street 54868
Mailing address: P.O. Box 232
  Rice Lake, WI 54868

Sheboygan

Coca-Cola Bottling Co. of
  Wisconsin
  Sheboygan Sales Center
1837 North Avenue 53081

Wausau

Coca-Cola Bottling Midwest, Inc.
1930 Grand Avenue 54401

WYOMING

Rock Springs

Rock Springs-Casper Coca-Cola
  Bottling Company, Inc.
1762 Blairtown Road 82902
Mailing address: P.O. Box 939
  Rock Springs, WY 82902
307/382-2233

Index